LETTERS of HOPE from PEOPLE of FAITH

AMERICAN VALUES
RELIGIOUS VOICES

★

AMERICAN VALUES

Letters of Hope from People of Faith

RELIGIOUS VOICES

VOLUME 2

About the University of Cincinnati Press

The University of Cincinnati Press is committed to publishing rigorous, peer reviewed, leading scholarship accessibly to stimulate dialog and erase disciplinary boundaries between the academy, public intellectuals and lay practitioners. Building on the university's longstanding tradition of social responsibility, the press publishes books on topics which expose and resolve disparities at every level of society and have local, national and global impact.

University of Cincinnati Press, Cincinnati 45221
© 2023

ISBN 978-1-947602-91-5 (hardback)
ISBN 978-1-947602-90-8 (e-book, PDF)

Library of Congress Cataloging-in-Publication data

Weiss, Andrea L. and Lisa M. Weinberger, editors.
American values, religious voices : 100 days, 100 letters / edited by Andrea L. Weiss and Lisa M. Weinberger.
Cincinnati : University of Cincinnati Press, 2019. | Identifiers: LCCN 2018034409 (print) | LCCN 2018041311
    (ebook) | ISBN 9781947602410 (Ebook, PDF) | ISBN 9781947602403 (hardback)
LCSH: United States—Religion—Miscellanea. | Values—United States—Miscellanea. | United States—Politics
    and government,—2017—Miscellanea. | Political culture—United States—History—21st century—Miscellanea.
    | Letters. | Public opinion—United States. | Trump, Donald, 1946–
LCC BL2525 (ebook) | LCC BL2525 .A547 2018 (print) | DDC 200.973—dc23
LC record available at https://lccn.loc.gov/2018034409

Designed and produced for UC Press by Masters Group Design • Philadelphia
Printed in the United States of America

First Printing

THIS BOOK

*is an invitation
to engage with diverse scholars,
to grapple with religious and national values,
and to think deeply about
what it means to be American.*

THE LETTERS

Read It Again

The Impact of the 2021 American
Values, Religious Voices Campaign

Prophetic Voices and Shifting Values

A Historian's Perspective

★ THE LETTERS IN PRACTICE ★

INDEXES

DAYS 61-70

DAYS 71-80

DAYS 81-90

DAYS 91-100

AMERICAN VALUES

Empathy

LETTERS: 19, 41, 49, 52, 54, 56, 72, 78, 89, 94

····· 18 LETTERS ON ·····

Compassion

LETTERS: 2, 13, 15, 16, 28, 51, 56, 59, 64, 65, 67, 71, 78, 80, 81, 88, 89, 94

····· 8 LETTERS ON ·····

Freedom

LETTERS: 21, 38, 43, 55, 73, 88, 91, 96

····· 6 LETTERS ON ·····

Diversity

LETTERS: 18, 51, 68, 77, 83, 100

····· 5 LETTERS ON ·····

Kindness

LETTERS: 12, 18, 56, 58, 91

····· 9 LETTERS ON ·····

Dignity

LETTERS: 6, 35, 43, 44, 53, 65, 87, 93, 94

····· 7 LETTERS ON ·····

Equity

LETTERS: 1, 16, 39, 69, 72, 91, 100

····· 7 LETTERS ON ·····

Common Good

LETTERS: 5, 21, 37, 48, 68, 74, 91

····· 7 LETTERS ON ·····

Respect

LETTERS: 9, 12, 18, 65, 87, 94, 100

····· 19 LETTERS ON ·····

Healing

LETTERS: 1, 4, 14, 19, 20, 24, 29, 32, 33, 36, 46, 52, 53, 56, 64, 73, 78, 87, 88

AMERICAN VALUES

····· 6 LETTERS ON ·····

Equality

LETTERS: 53, 64,
72, 88, 89, 93

····· 39 LETTERS ON ·····

Justice

LETTERS: 1, 2, 3, 4, 5, 7, 10, 20, 23,
24, 25, 26, 28, 30, 36, 39, 43, 50, 51,
54, 57, 58, 59, 63, 64, 69, 71, 72, 76, 77,
78, 81, 87, 88, 91, 94, 96, 99, 100

····· 27 LETTERS ON ·····

Hope

LETTERS: 1, 15, 16, 18, 20,
22, 26, 28, 29, 31, 39, 40, 41,
45, 51, 56, 58, 62, 63, 67, 68,
81, 82, 88, 93, 99, 100

····· 7 LETTERS ON ·····

Unity

LETTERS: 20, 24, 28, 60,
64, 73, 83

····· 9 LETTERS ON ·····

Mercy

LETTERS: 3, 7, 11, 23, 24, 26, 28, 58, 71

····· 20 LETTERS ON ·····

Love

LETTERS: 2, 3, 12, 20, 21, 22, 26, 28, 42, 46, 58, 62, 65, 71, 73, 75, 76, 79, 80, 89

····· 4 LETTERS ON ·····

Generosity

LETTERS: 32, 56, 69, 91

····· 18 LETTERS ON ·····

Peace

LETTERS: 1, 3, 4, 7, 24, 25, 28, 40, 41, 48, 50, 51, 53, 59, 71, 79, 87, 97

····· 25 LETTERS ON ·····

Truth

LETTERS: 3, 4, 5, 9, 12, 18, 28, 29, 33, 47, 53, 54, 58, 62, 63, 64, 72, 73, 82, 85, 86, 87, 89, 95, 100

····· 12 LETTERS ON ·····

Courage

LETTERS: 1, 19, 20, 22, 26, 33, 37, 54, 56, 64, 74, 79

Keep the Letters Coming

★ ★ ★

The Origin of American Values, Religious Voices

By Andrea L. Weiss

Tuesday, November 3, 2020—Election Day— came and went. So did Wednesday, Thursday, Friday. Still no declared winner. As states counted and recounted their ballots, I started composing a letter in my head. While we did not yet know who our next president would be, we knew how polarized our country remained. No matter who would be sworn in on January 20, we knew we still were confronting a devastating pandemic and reckoning with a pervasive legacy of racism and an imperiled planet. I had a letter to our leaders in Washington that I wanted to write, and I sensed both that other scholars of religion might have something to say and that people across the country might want to listen.

Why would the 2020 presidential election move me to think about writing a letter? The answer to that question goes back four years, again to the days following the conclusion of one of our most consequential national elections.

While I was walking my dog on Friday, November 11, 2016—just three days after the election of Donald Trump—an idea started to form. Months of provocative rhetoric and audacious campaign promises had left me wondering what happened to "liberty and justice for all" or "Give me your tired, your poor, you huddled masses yearning to breathe free." News footage of violence breaking out at campaign rallies and tales of families torn apart by politics had made me question what happened to "Love your neighbor as yourself" or the notion of all humans being created in God's image.

Meandering through my neighborhood on that fall afternoon in 2016, I thought to myself: Maybe Bible scholars like me have something to say at this fraught moment in our nation's history. Maybe our politicians—particularly those who profess to come to elected office with strong religious commitments—need to hear from those of us who dedicate our lives to understanding the ancient sources of wisdom that are filled with enduring truths about what is right and just. Maybe, I thought, everyone in our country could benefit from that wisdom, especially at a time when many people were feeling unmoored and anxious, uncertain of where we were headed as a nation.

So that gave me an idea: What if I could get 100 scholars of religion—people across the country of all faiths and backgrounds—to write a letter a day to the president, vice president, and members of Congress, reflecting on our core American values that connect to our different religious traditions?

Before my far-fetched idea could dissipate, I consulted with my neighbor and mentor, Mark S. Smith, Helena Professor of Old Testament Literature and Exegesis at Princeton Theological Seminary. After I knocked on his door and hesitantly shared my nascent vision of gathering 100 colleagues to write letters to the new administration, he said, "I think it's a good idea, and I'll help you."

To secure the financial backing for the project, I next spoke to Rabbi Aaron Panken, of blessed memory, then president of Hebrew Union College–Jewish Institute of Religion (HUC-JIR). Rabbi Panken enthusiastically supported what would become American Values, Religious Voices because he wanted the faculty at HUC-JIR to be thought leaders, applying our scholarly expertise to address the most pressing issues of our day.

To actualize my idea, I contacted my friend Lisa Weinberger, creative director and founder of Masters Group Design in Philadelphia, and asked for her help to design a visual identity and other graphic assets the project might involve. Lisa responded right away: "I'm in." She later explained that after the election, she felt like she had a hole in her heart. But what could she do as a graphic designer that would make a difference? Then my email ended up in her inbox, offering her a way to volunteer her talents and resources for the sake of the greater good and a way to respond to the negativity of the campaign with something positive. Together, we created the national, nonpartisan campaign called American Values, Religious Voices: 100 Days, 100 Letters.

I then formed a multifaith advisory committee that included Deirdre Good (then theologian in residence at Trinity Church Wall Street), Herbert Robinson Marbury (associate professor of Bible and the ancient Near East at Vanderbilt University Divinity School), Hussein Rashid (an independent scholar and founder of islamicate, L3C), Mark S. Smith, and Elsie R. Stern (then vice president for academic affairs and associate professor of Bible at the Reconstructionist Rabbinical College). The advisory committee finalized the contours of the project and sent out an initial round of nearly a hundred invitations on December 2, 2016.

In the invitation, we explained to potential letter writers:

"This project aims to contribute
constantly to our national discourse, reaffirming who we are as Americans and modeling how we can learn from one another and work together for the common good."

We asked people: "What passages from your religious tradition have you been thinking about in the wake of the election? What issues most concern you, and how does your religious heritage speak to those concerns? What message—rooted in the texts you study and teach—would you most like to deliver to our national leaders and to a wider interfaith audience, many of whom long for guidance, inspiration, and a reaffirmation of what it means to be an American?" We concluded the invitation with a message that summarized what the project aimed to accomplish: "Individually, it is hard to feel that one can have an impact on events unfolding around us. Collectively, we have the potential to speak truthfully and powerfully to those making critical decisions about our nation's future."

Starting with the first day of Donald Trump's presidency and running for 100 days, we disseminated each day's letter in a variety of ways. At five o'clock each morning, we emailed a letter to our *explicit* audience: the president, vice president, the chiefs of staff and legislative directors of the members of the 115th Congress, plus select members of the Trump administration. At the same time, day after day, each letter was uploaded to our website for our *implicit* audience: the more than 2,000 subscribers who received an early morning email with a link to the letter, as well as the many others who learned about the letters through daily posts on our social media platforms. In addition, with my dog in tow, every morning I walked to my nearby post office and mailed two printed and stamped letters, one individually addressed to the president and the other to the vice president.

> ## The letters … "created dialogue and healing."

Once we started sending the letters, readers began contacting us to share their feedback. People told us they read the letters like a morning prayer or a daily meditation. They told us how much they valued hearing from unaccustomed voices and appreciated the expanding "archive of compassion and democracy" that offered "sustenance and courage from deep ancient wells." They told us the letters made them feel they were not alone.

One campaign follower, a Democrat in Manhattan, told us how during the presidential campaign, he had stopped speaking with his brother, a staunch Republican in Tulsa, Oklahoma. The letters provided a means of reconciliation and, in his own words, "created dialogue and healing." The one recipient in Washington who replied to our letters, Katherine McGuire, then chief of staff for the Illinois Republican Congressman Randy Hultgren, wrote on Day 24 (February 12, 2017): "Keep the letters coming. People are reading them. They help to make sense of the world we live in today and remind us of the world we all want to live in tomorrow."

By all measures, the campaign exceeded our expectations. It culminated in the publication of the 100 letters, along with four accompanying essays, in a 2019 book published by the University of Cincinnati Press entitled *American Values, Religious Voices: 100 Days, 100 Letters.*

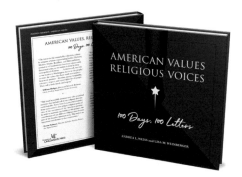

With that, I thought the campaign was finished—until the 2020 election took place. As we waited nearly a week for the election results, I started to think that we needed another 100 letters.

Realistic about my capacity to carry out the campaign given my current role as provost of HUC-JIR, I contacted my daughter, Rebecca Tauber, then a senior history and English major at Williams College, and asked her to work with me as editorial assistant. She quickly recruited two other Williams students: Kayla Gillman as creative assistant and Sophia Sonnenfeldt as communications assistant. Lisa Weinberger agreed to manage the website renovation and help guide and support the project.

On December 2, 2020, I emailed all 100 of the 2017 Values & Voices letter writers. I explained: "Four years ago, following the election of Donald Trump, I invited you to take part in an effort to bring together scholars from diverse religious traditions to write to our national leaders about the core values that have grounded and guided our nation. . . . Four years later, as we contend with a pandemic and a deeply divided country, I remain convinced that scholars of religion and the texts we teach can speak with wisdom and urgency to this precarious, precious moment in our nation's history." That same day, a quarter of the recipients responded, thanking me for launching the campaign again and enthusiastically committing to write a new letter. In the end, we enlisted fifty-nine returning letter writers and forty-two new scholars (with one co-authored letter).

The 2021 campaign operated just like the first had in 2017, with 100 daily letters sent to our elected leaders in Washington and over 2,000 subscribers, with many other people reading and responding to the letters on social media. The key difference was that this time around the letters were addressed:

Dear President Biden, Vice President Harris, and Members of the 117th Congress.

An upgrade of the original website allowed the 2021 Values & Voices campaign to showcase the manifold backgrounds and perspectives of the letter writers in new ways. We invited authors to make a video or audio recording of themselves reading their letters, which we posted above the written text on the website and collected on our YouTube channel. Being able to listen to the letter writers' voices and watch them in their homes or offices added color and flavor to the letters, further highlighting the varied perspectives and personalities brought together for this project.

★ VALUES & VOICES ON YOUTUBE ★

Letter 95: Kelly Brown Douglas

Letter 94: Raj Nadella

Letter 92: Dawn M. Nothwehr

Letter 89: Nikky-Guninder Kaur Singh

Letter 85: Christopher Key Chapple

Letter 84: Shreena Niketa Gandhi

Letter 81: Efrain Agosto

Letter 76: Aristotle Papanikolaou

Letter 65: Grace Song

Thanks to the initiative of Philadelphia-based arts leader, educator, and consultant David Bradley, we organized "'Dear President Biden': A Presidents' Day Performance & Community Conversation," a live Zoom event that offered another means to engage our community in this public conversation about politics and religion. On February 15, 2021, over 300 people gathered at our virtual public square to listen to actors David Strathairn, Nilaja Sun, Taysha Canales, Angel Desai, and Michele Tauber perform selected letters. Songwriters Keisha Hutchins and Ami Yares with Bethlehem the Vocussionist sang original songs inspired by the letters.

The program also included a recent immigrant and college student reading a letter, remarks by Congressman Dwight Evans of Pennsylvania, and a discussion among committed citizens from across the country. The lyrics of Hutchins's song (see page 162) captured the spirit of the event and of the campaign as a whole: "We are bound, bound up in you, bound up in me, we are bound. Born of one truth, that sets us free, we are bound . . . What once started with me now ends with you. We are bound."

Dear President Biden

Scan to watch the Presidents' Day Performance & Community Conversation

Using a similar format, we marked Women's History Month on March 30, 2021, by assembling a diverse panel of female-identified authors—Jacqueline Hidalgo, Lia Howard, Nirinjan Kaur Khalsa-Baker, Karoline Lewis and Kimberly Russaw—who read their letters and reflected on the contribution of women to this project and religion and politics more broadly. This online event—called "'Excuse Me, I'm Speaking': A Multifaith Gathering of Scholars Reading and Reflecting on Values & Voices Letters Penned by Women"—enabled authors and campaign followers to be in conversation with one another, thus transforming the written word into an opportunity for civic dialogue.

"Excuse me, I'm speaking."

A Multifaith Gathering of Scholars Reading and Reflecting on Values & Voices Letters Penned by Women / March 30, 8 PM ET

Presented by the American Values, Religious Voices Campaign

These events not only brought people together during the first year of the pandemic, but they helped garner media attention for the 2021 campaign, which was covered in *The Washington Post*, BBC Radio 4, *The Forward*, *The San Diego Union-Tribune*, *The Philadelphia Citizen*, and other media outlets.

Throughout the 100 days, as more people learned about the campaign and helped expand its impact, we received copious feedback that documented how our followers experienced the daily letters. The positive response proved that four years later, people valued the second batch of letters as much as the first. The potential remains for these letters to be a force for good in a fractured world. ★

Andrea L. Weiss
Jack, Joseph and Morton Mandel Provost & Associate Professor of Bible, Hebrew Union College–Jewish Institute of Religion

Read It Again

★ ★ ★

The Impact of the 2021 American Values, Religious Voices Campaign

By Rebecca Tauber

On January 20, 2021, about ten days into the launch of American Values, Religious Voices, Rabbi Daniel Zemel had a new morning routine:

1. Go downstairs
2. Turn on the coffee
3. Bring in the newspaper from the driveway— BUT DON'T TAKE IT OUT OF THE PLASTIC BAG!
4. Sit down in the kitchen (Who does that when every morning in a hurry?)
5. Smell the coffee
6. Read the Values and Voices Letter
7. Read it again
8. Think/learn
9. Select a phrase to read out loud.
10. Get the coffee.

Zemel was not the only person who told us that they reshaped their morning rituals around the Values & Voices letter in their inbox. One reader swapped her daily news diet for the day's letter. "They became a different 'season of devotion' for me, like a Lenten discipline," she wrote in a survey asking for feedback on the project. "No matter how tempted I was to open *The New York Times* or *Washington Post*, the letter was first. It became my morning devotion, setting my frame for the day."

In a year marked by endless doomscrolling, inboxes clogged with emails requiring just a bit too much energy to answer, and the direct wake of the January 6 insurrection, the Values & Voices campaign provided stability. Every morning, the letters "set a framework for [the] day," according to one reader. They provided hope rather than despair.

Like the 2017 project, which had seen one governmental reaction from Katherine McGuire, chief of staff for Illinois Republican Congressman Randy Hultgren, the response from our explicit audience—the president, vice president, and members of Congress—was limited. Congressman Dwight Evans of Pennsylvania joined Values & Voices on Zoom for "'Dear President Biden': A Presidents' Day Performance & Community Conversation" to offer his thoughts about civic engagement. Several months after the campaign ended, we received a handful of identical letters from Vice President Kamala Harris's office, addressed to different writers, thanking them for their support.

But still, the letters echoed. They reached people around the world, as our over 2,000 subscribers and hundreds of social media followers forwarded the letters to family and friends, used them in classes, quoted them in worship services, and found themselves going back to reread favorites. People visited our website from Canada, the UK, India, South Korea, China, Israel, Singapore, Hong Kong, Germany, and more. During President Joe Biden's first 100 days, almost 30,000 people visited **ValuesandVoices.com**, where they could read the letters, subscribe to the project, and learn more about the writers.

Yet statistics only tell a fraction of the story. In feedback solicited at the conclusion of the project, many readers wrote of how the letters brought them hope in a divided and tumultuous moment. "Nowadays a person can often feel they are alone, shouting into a void that will eventually swallow them too," one campaign follower wrote. "It is lovely that you found a way to strengthen and enhance many voices with a shared goal: shedding light and sharing perspective."

Another subscriber agreed: "Each letter inspires hope for what at times seems impossible." One follower shared: "These letters gave me hope for the future, not just by their thoughtful content, but in knowing that there are so many religious scholars thinking and writing deeply about the spiritual foundation of America."

For author Shreena Niketa Gandhi (Letter 84), the letters helped her maintain hope in the positive power of faith: "Reading those letters reminded me that I'm not alone, and that religion has an immense power not just for oppression, but also liberation."

> *Each letter inspires hope for what at times seems impossible.*

The sense of hope and inspiration sparked by the American Values, Religious Voices campaign came not just from the content of the letters, but from the diversity of the letter writers.

Rabbi Zemel appreciated that the letters gave him a new friend every morning. "These letters brought the America that I love to me in a way that was soulful, deep, and learned," he observed. "The America that I love is a place where when I am waiting in line to pay for my groceries the person in front of me is from one country, the person behind me is from a different country and the person working at the counter from a third."

With Buddhist, Christian, Hindu, Jewish, Muslim, and Sikh writers of different denominations, races, and ethnicities, the letters brought this grocery store line to readers across the world. "I looked at these letters as an opportunity to learn how people different than myself

> ## *Values & Voices helped people feel like they were part of something larger than themselves.*

"look at the world," an anonymous reader wrote. "I am an older white woman who has been brought up knowing that I will be treated with respect and that I have a voice in this world. It is clear from what one sees on the news, that many [did] not grow up with that same sense of belonging and ease." Another reader similarly reflected: "As a white Christian, I seldom hear the ideas of women, women of color, male and female Jewish rabbis, and Muslim men and women. It was encouraging and hopeful to read the thoughts of so many people concerned with the common good."

The 2021 iteration of American Values, Religious Voices took place in the middle of a pandemic that brought long-lasting inequities in the U.S. into stark relief. The campaign started eight months after the murder of George Floyd and the subsequent months of protest and racial reckoning that spread throughout the country. In a moment that forced those with privilege—particularly white Americans—to grapple with their understanding of race and justice, Values & Voices provided a way to understand others from different backgrounds, experiences, and perspectives. And, in the wake of a violent assault on democracy witnessed in Washington, D.C., on January 6, 2021, the letters brought hope, presenting a range of answers to the ever-pressing question of who we are as a nation.

In an already divided country, the COVID-19 pandemic put up even more barriers to dialogue and understanding. As the world was forced to shift online, it was easy to fall into internet echo chambers, and

opportunities to join Zemel's grocery store line in person were few and far between.

For the authors who wrote letters in 2017 and 2021, the subscribers who followed the campaign both times, and the many others who read or listened to the letters in various forms, Values & Voices helped people feel like they were part of something larger than themselves. The project brought people a sense of connection to other writers and readers, to the values articulated in the letters, to the ancient religious texts offering sorely sought-after wisdom.

This book aims to extend this sense of connection. This volume collects the 100 letters from 2021, arranged in chapters of ten, just as we did in the first volume of the 2017 letters. You can read the letters sequentially, as they appeared from Day 1 on January 20 to Day 100 on April 29, 2021. Or you can explore the letters by subject or by author, using the "American Values" pages in the front of the book (pages 8–11), the pages that conclude each chapter of ten letters with a compilation of quotes about a some of the most prominent values, or the index in the back. Volume 2 also adds a set of essays on how to use the letters in practical settings, including education, political activism, the arts, and more.

This book is an invitation to engage with diverse scholars, to grapple with religious and national values, and to think deeply about what it means to be American. As we wrote to our subscribers at the launch of the 2021 campaign: We hope you will join us. ★

Rebecca Tauber
Journalist and Values & Voices
Editorial Assistant

Prophetic Voices and Shifting Values

★ ★ ★

A Historian's Perspective

By Casey Bohlen

In November 2016, Bible professor Rabbi Andrea L. Weiss and graphic designer Lisa Weinberger launched the first American Values, Religious Voices campaign. Donald Trump had just been elected to the U.S. presidency, on the heels of a campaign marked by inflammatory rhetoric, deliberate misinformation, virulent xenophobia, and allegations of sexual assault. Weiss was understandably disturbed. The incoming administration practiced a politics that, in her words, disregarded many of "the core values that had grounded and guided our country in the past." She conceived of the campaign as a corrective, a chance for leading religious scholars "to remind [themselves]—and us—of who we are as a nation."

The letters did that, and more: they also offered a vision of who we ought to be. Even as the 2017 American Values, Religious Voices campaign reflected core American values, it also sought to shape them, to shift them, to elevate them to a higher plane. The 2021 Values & Voices campaign, directed at the incoming Biden administration, carried a similar weight. Its letters offered prophetic meditations on our public life, cataloging our moral shortcomings even as they offered hope for a redemptive future.

Such projects have a long lineage in American history, especially in moments of acute crisis. Amidst the upheaval of the American Revolution, clergy drew from religious wells to build national unity, envisioning Christianity as a source for the virtues necessary for self-government. Faced with the bloodshed of the Civil War, President Abraham Lincoln brought religious values to bear on the nation's suffering, interpreting violence as a divine scourge for the sin of slavery, yet holding out hope for reconciliation through the better angels of our nature. Following the rise of fascism and the outbreak of World War II, scholars like Jewish sociologist Will Herberg and Catholic philosopher Fr. John F. Cronin reimagined "Judeo-Christianity" as a democratic bulwark against totalitarianism, holding forth in interfaith meetings with such names as the National Conference on the Spiritual Foundations of American Democracy and the Conference on Science, Philosophy and Religion in Their Relation to the Democratic Way of Life, Inc.

Yet even as the American Values, Religious Voices campaign follows in these footsteps, it treads new ground, responding to the crises of our current historical moment in at least three distinctive ways.

1. Acting in Solidarity

First, well over a third of the 2021 letters call on readers to act in political and moral solidarity with the vulnerable, the needy, and the oppressed. Their theological sources vary. Eric Daryl Meyer (Letter 57) grounds his message in Catholic social teaching, with its "preferential option for the poor." Hamza M. Zafer (Letter 97) draws upon the Qur'an's demand that we redistribute our surplus to "the deprived and the displaced, the petitioner and the enslaved." Kenneth Ngwa (Letter 69) uses the Exodus story, emphasizing the pivotal role of midwives Shiphrah and Puah in liberating the Israelites from slavery. Whatever their inspiration, these authors are committed to a politics of justice, conceived of as restorative action on behalf of minoritized communities. And they frame that pursuit as a divine commandment: *tzedek tzedek tirdof,* as Marc Z. Brettler (Letter 4) cites, quoting Deuteronomy 16:20: "After justice, after justice, you must chase."

> *… these authors are committed to a politics of justice, conceived of as restorative action on behalf of minoritized communities.*

And no wonder. We live in an age of extraordinary material abundance, yet economic inequality has sharpened to levels not seen since the 1920s. It has been half a century since the federal government broke the back of Jim Crow and declared reproductive autonomy a constitutional right; yet recent Supreme Court decisions have given states the license to criminalize abortion and restrict voting access once again. Public support for racial and gender equality has never been higher, yet horrific incidents of racial and sexual violence punctuate our news cycle with regularity. We live in a moment when the gap between our nation's professed ideals and its realities seems unusually glaring. Jeremiads are tailor-made for such moments. Many of these letters take up that mantle, offering biting critiques of American hypocrisy and a clarion call to restorative action. In the process, they ground that action in a politics of solidarity, demanding that readers conceive of their task as more than mere charity—that they "weep with [their] aggrieved siblings" (Letter 82), as Jesus wept for Lazarus.

2. The Common Good

That emphasis on solidarity also surfaces in a second, and closely related, theme. One-third of the letter writers make "the common good" central to their moral vision. They tend to ground that emphasis in scriptural commandments that demand "love for neighbor and stranger," as Tamara Cohn Eskenazi and Jacob L. Wright (Letter 22) put it. Visions for what that love looks like in practice vary. Shalom E. Holtz (Letter 34) relies on kinship metaphors, calling on us to "transform

> *One-third of the letter writers make "the common good" central to their moral vision.*

our world from neighborhood into family." Love L. Sechrest (Letter 73) deploys corporeal metaphors, drawing on Ephesians to describe the public as a body, bound together by the "ligaments" of good leadership.

Whatever the metaphor, their collective message demands that readers look beyond their "self-centered ego" (Letter 53), that they "think of a politics beyond the contractual" (Letter 76), and that they build "cultures of collective responsibility" (Letter 37) capable of fostering a "beloved community" (Letter 28).

Again, this theme feels distinctively urgent in our current historical moment. The past half century has been marked by the rise of an individualistic ethos. From the demise of the welfare state to the ascendance of neoliberalism to the fraying of civic organizational life, a thinned-out vision of an isolated "I," standing apart from society, has gradually replaced a thicker vision of a collective "we." In reaction, these letters work to decenter the self and meditate upon our mutual obligations to each other and to society. Such a perspective is not new per se. Precedents can be found as far back as the colonial era, when John Winthrop also described the community as a body knit together by the "ligaments" of love, and declared that if one member suffers, all suffer with it. But it feels freshly urgent in our moment, as we reap the whirlwind of social disintegration produced by decades of countervailing trends.

3. Diversity and Pluralism

Coursing through and underneath those two themes comes a third: a commitment to diversity and pluralism as the path by which we might secure justice and build community. It is here that this project breaks most firmly with the past. Historically, there has been a tight connection between the religious construction of a moral or national center, on the one hand, and the persecution of those who find themselves outside of it, on the other. Advocates of Christian virtue in the early national period did help to bind the nation together. They also passed blasphemy laws and religious tests for office meant to exclude and persecute non-Protestants, many of which remain on the books (if unenforceable) today. The more expansive vision of America as a "Judeo-Christian" nation that was constructed in the wake of World War II helped to mute anti-Catholic and anti-Semitic impulses. It also underpinned "Red Scare" purges of religious, political, and sexual nonconformists.

… this project's title uses the plural. It captures religious voices. It articulates American values.

Tellingly, those postwar predecessors used the definite article in the unwieldy titles of the conferences mentioned earlier. They sought the spiritual foundations of American democracy. They defended the democratic way of life. Their efforts to forge a center frequently involved the erasure of difference. Their invocation of a "Judeo-Christian nation" signaled unity through language that melded together traditions. They invoked a lowest-common-denominator spirituality, rendered so vague as to be almost meaningless, most famously seen with President Eisenhower's declaration that "our form of government has no sense unless it is founded in a deeply felt religious faith, and I don't care what it is."

By contrast, this project's title uses the plural. It captures religious voices. It articulates American values. And in contrast to earlier historical moments, its roster of contributors is astoundingly diverse. Their ranks include Hindus and Muslims, Buddhists and Sikhs, Quakers and Mormons. In a country long dominated by Protestant Christianity, about three-fifths of these letter writers are non-Protestant, and over two-fifths are non-Christian. Nearly a quarter hail from outside the Christian and Jewish traditions altogether. Those numbers capture only the religious diversity of these authors, who also represent a wide range of racial and regional perspectives, on top of the more ephemeral aspects of identity that make up each of our multitudinous selves.

That diversity is itself a barometer of a deeper transformation, which inheres in the language and perspectives structuring most of the letters. Very few letters speak of "religion" holistically, as if such a thing exists outside of the particularities of specific traditions. By contrast, most authors ground their moral vision in a particular religious identity, writing "as an American Muslim" (Letter 24), or "as a Jewish ethicist" (Letter 60), or "from the Christian tradition" (Letter 57), or in light of "my Sikh faith" (Letter 2).

The authors' specificity is perhaps unsurprising, given that every letter is addressed to a multifaith audience. But there are many ways to speak to such an audience. A majority of these authors do so by positioning their faith as particularistic and embodied, rather than universal or universalizable. They name their experiences and traditions, offering them up to the reader as one tool among many, rather than conflating their identities and beliefs with "religion" or "morality"

> **"**
> *[The authors] approach the public sphere with humility and grace, modeling dialogue across difference, and unity without erasure.*

writ large. They shun exceptionalism. They refuse to regress to a lowest-common-denominator spirituality. And in doing so, they approach the public sphere with humility and grace, modeling dialogue across difference, and unity without erasure. As our nation becomes increasingly diverse, and populist resistance to that diversity becomes increasingly virulent, we need such models now more than ever.

What, then, can these letters and their themes tell us about who we are as a nation and what "core values" define our own time?

In my more optimistic moments, I am tempted to suggest that the pendulum is swinging, that the values of justice, community, and pluralism are on the rise, and that Trumpism is no more than the reactionary gasp that comes with every tide of change. Yet it is worth remembering that the American Values, Religious Voices campaign—explicitly, self-consciously, and with very good reason—solicited only the voices of religious scholars. Every single letter-writer in this campaign holds an advanced degree. Nearly all of them are employed in higher education.

I do not offer that fact as a criticism. Indeed, I see it as a virtue. Too often of late, academic credentialing has been treated as a shortcoming, rather than a strength. It is refreshing to see scholars singled out and honored for their expertise, to see learnedness treated as a sign of wisdom and insight, to see a campaign devote itself to bridging the gap between the "ivory tower" and the broader public sphere. In a world of "alternative facts," that goal should be frankly celebrated. (Or so I believe, being myself a credentialed academic.)

Yet the campaign's emphasis on scholars does make it hard to draw conclusions about the core values of our time more generally. Today, among ordinary Americans, there is in fact an inverse relationship between religiosity (by a certain definition, anyway) and the values that define these letters. The more religiously active and orthodox Americans are—as indicated by their certainty in the existence of God, the self-described importance of religion in their life, or the frequency with which

American Voices by Benjamin Brown

they attend religious services, for instance—the more likely they are to oppose same-sex marriage, to say that government aid to the poor does more harm than good, and to believe that stricter environmental laws and regulations cost too many jobs and hurt the economy.

Almost every single letter in the 2021 campaign positions itself either implicitly or explicitly against the outgoing Trump administration. Yet in the 2020 election, President Trump won the vote of 59 percent of American citizens who attend religious services at least monthly, and an astonishing 71 percent of white Americans who attend religious services at least monthly.

The hope driving this project is that the values incarnated in these letters will point the way toward a brighter future.

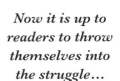

Now it is up to readers to throw themselves into the struggle…

The reality is that a competing set of values—exclusionary rather than inclusive, chauvinistic rather than particularistic, white nationalist rather than pluralist—have just as strong a claim to the title of "American values." And their advocates are committed not to fostering civil discourse in the public square, but to seizing that square for their own.

Yet, as noted at the start of this essay, the virtue of this campaign lies not only in its effort to capture who we are as a nation, but also in its prophetic vision of who we ought to be. The words contained in these pages may not be enough to get us there. But they are a start. Now it is up to readers to throw themselves into the struggle, to embrace Jacqueline M. Hidalgo's (Letter 45) call to "build a bridge to a future that reckons with the past but refuses to resemble it," and to make sure that these words become more than mere words. ★

Casey Bohlen, PhD
Mellon Visiting Assistant Professor in History and Public Discourse
Smith College

THE
LETTERS

RELIGIOUS VOICES: DAYS 1–10

LETTER 1 | JANUARY 20, 2021

Andrea L. Weiss

Jack, Joseph and Morton Mandel Provost & Associate Professor of Bible, Hebrew Union College–Jewish Institute of Religion

LETTER 2 | JANUARY 21, 2021

Simran Jeet Singh

Visiting Professor, Union Theological Seminary

LETTER 3 | JANUARY 22, 2021

Lisa Bowens

Associate Professor of New Testament, Princeton Theological Seminary

LETTER 4 | JANUARY 23, 2021

Marc Z. Brettler

Bernice and Morton Lerner Distinguished Professor of Jewish Studies, Duke University

LETTER 5 | JANUARY 24, 2021

Anantanand Rambachan

Professor of Religion, Philosophy, and Asian Studies, Saint Olaf College

LETTER 6 | JANUARY 25, 2021

Carmen M. Nanko-Fernández

Professor of Hispanic Theology and Ministry Director, Hispanic Theology and Ministry Program, Catholic Theological Union

LETTER 7 | JANUARY 26, 2021

Hussein Rashid

Founder, islamicate, L3C

LETTER 8 | JANUARY 27, 2021

Nadia Kizenko

Professor of History, Director of Religious Studies, State University of New York, Albany

LETTER 9 | JANUARY 28, 2021

Murali Balaji

Founder, Maruthi Education Consulting

LETTER 10 | JANUARY 29, 2021

Judith Plaskow

Professor Emerita of Religious Studies, Manhattan College

Andrea L. Weiss

Dear President Biden, Vice President Harris, and Members of the 117th Congress,

As you begin your service to our fragile, fractured country, the challenges you face seem almost insurmountable. How will you achieve the lofty goals that motivated you to run for office amidst a devastating pandemic, assaults on our democracy, the corrosive effects of systemic racism, and ample evidence of an imperiled planet?

The word for "hope" in the Hebrew Bible offers an answer. Psalm 27 ends with the charge, repeated twice, to hope for God (v. 14). The same verb appears when Job exclaims: "I hoped for good, but evil came" (Job 30:2); and when the people lament: "Why do we hope for peace, but there is no good; for a time of healing, but behold there is terror?" (Jeremiah 14:19). The verb recurs in Isaiah 5:7, an ancient verse with a contemporary resonance: God "hoped for justice, but behold, injustice; for equity, but behold, iniquity."

> "
> *Be hopeful about your ability to bring about a better world.*

In these and other citations, hope leads to disappointment when an anticipated positive outcome fails to come to fruition. The Rev. Dr. Martin Luther King Jr. recognized the relationship between hope and disappointment in an address delivered on February 6, 1968, when he declared: "We must accept finite disappointment but never lose infinite hope."

How can we hold both hope and disappointment, in our own lives and in your work as our elected leaders? In between the two calls to hope for God in Psalm 27, we find a phrase sometimes translated as: "Be strong and be of good courage." Elsewhere in the Bible, the two roots in this verse are used as part of an expression of encouragement, as when Moses charges Joshua: "Be strong and courageous" (Deuteronomy 31:7). But only in Psalm 27:14 and Psalm 31:25 does the second verb appear in the causative grammatical form, which I would translate as: "Be strong and cause your heart to be resilient."

Take that advice to heart as you get to work. Be courageous. Be kind. Be hopeful about your ability to bring about a better world.

Dear President Biden, Vice President Harris, and Members of the 117th Congress,

Thank you for your leadership. And thank you for your service.

Often, these two concepts—leadership and service—are taken separately, as two discrete ways of engaging with the world around us. We typically think of leadership as how someone with power influences those who follow them, and service as a way of supporting those without power.

What my Sikh faith has taught me, though, is that the two go hand in hand: We each have our own forms of power, and we can each deploy that power for the betterment of our world. This is servant-leadership.

I have learned that leadership is at its best when it is rooted in compassion and humility. The poorest leaders are those who work for their own gain and seek to serve themselves. The greatest leaders are those who are connected to their people and work for the benefit of those they serve. One approach is self-centered and leads to disconnection, while the other is inspired by love and produces justice. We have seen with our own eyes the difference between the two.

> *...leadership is at its best when it is rooted in compassion and humility.*

In the Sikh tradition, we refer to this selfless, love-inspired service as *seva*. It is both the natural expression of our love and the practice for cultivating love. Service, we believe, is the goal and the practice. We believe this because service itself is love.

One of the most commonly sung praises of Guru Gobind Singh, the 10th Sikh guru, announces: "*vaho vaho gobind singh aapay gurchela.* Amazing, amazing is Gobind Singh, who is both the guru and the servant."

For Sikhs, this is not just empty praise. We aspire to each be like Guru Gobind Singh and to embody his qualities, including his unique approach to leadership—to lead and to serve in the same breath.

His approach to leadership as a form of service is an approach from which we all can learn. As we move toward building a more just and more loving world, we would all do well to follow in these footsteps.

DAY 3, LETTER 3   Lisa Bowens

Dear President Biden, Vice President Harris, and Members of the 117th Congress,

As I write this letter, simultaneous crises exist. A pandemic affects the physical, economic, mental, spiritual, and emotional health of our nation and the world. Over 400,000 Americans have died, bringing immense grief and trauma. The disturbing and frightening scenes of rioters storming Capitol Hill remain emblazoned upon many minds, for such actions threaten this republic's democratic ideals and norms. Racial divisions, which run deep in our nation, continue to plague us like a virus refusing eradication.

> *" *
>
> *Jesus reminds us not to neglect justice, mercy, faith, and love …*

Can Christian scripture speak to such crises? Words do matter; and for Christians, the Word matters. John's gospel calls Jesus the Word of God that became flesh and dwelled among us (John 1:14). Jesus, a Jew, lived in the midst of political corruption, deep divides between the rich and the poor, Roman oppression of the Jews, and sicknesses, like leprosy, for which there were no cure. Jesus' arrival reveals that God comes to humanity in times of crises and that God's care for and commitment to humanity and the world remain. Christ is Immanuel—meaning "God is with us" (Matthew 1:23)—a God who refuses to abandon us in the midst of a world filled with pain, hate, injustice, oppression, and division.

Jesus gives us words of comfort: "I am with you always" (Matthew 28:20) and "Peace, I leave with you; my peace I give to you" (John 14:27). His presence empowers participation with God's ways in the world, for God did not create people to destroy, hate, or abuse each other. Instead, we care for and love one another as Christ loves us (John 15:12). Jesus reminds us not to neglect justice, mercy, faith, and love, for these are integral, not optional or antithetical, to faith (Matthew 23:23).

Do we speak out against hate, do justice in an anti-justice world, proclaim truth in a world that craves fantasy? Yes. Christ's presence empowers and calls us to do what is right. Indeed, the Word matters. May we, in the words we speak and in the lives we live, reveal this reality. And may God's Spirit guide us all in the momentous days ahead.

DAY 4, LETTER 4   **Marc Z. Brettler**

Dear President Biden, Vice President Harris, and Members of the 117th Congress,

Four years ago, after the election results were announced, I wrote two biblical quotations in Hebrew on my office door, so that I would see them daily, be reminded of their truth, and be spurred to action.

The first was from Deuteronomy 16:20, which should be translated as: "After justice, after justice, must you chase" (*tzedek tzedek tirdof*). Most English translations miss how emphatic this command is. It repeats "justice" twice—as the medieval Jewish commentator Abraham ibn Ezra notes, this doubling implies that you must act justly time after time, whether it is to your advantage or disadvantage. The word I translated as "chase" is often incorrectly rendered less forcefully as "follow" or "pursue"—but it is a very physical "running" word. You do, and should, get tired from such sprinting—but it is essential to keep running after justice and to call out and to redress injustice, wherever you may find it.

> *May this administration use scriptures well, to chase justice and to love the truth …*

My second quote is more tranquil and aims to counterbalance the frenetic image of the first: "love truth and *shalom*" (Zechariah 8:19). While guiding the Jews to recover from a traumatic national calamity, the prophet Zechariah was an optimist, proclaiming in one of my favorite Bible passages: "There shall yet be old men and women in the squares of Jerusalem, each with staff in hand because of their great age. And the squares of the city shall be crowded with boys and girls playing in the squares" (Zechariah 8:4–5). But this new society must be based on truth and *shalom*. Typically that last word is translated as "peace," which we so desperately hope for in these turbulent times. But its meaning here is "personal well-being" or "wholeness"—the main responsibility of government. Only through such wholeness can the young and old enjoy and benefit from life.

I believe that sections of all the world's scriptures—including the Hebrew Bible, my scripture—have the ability to heal. May this administration use scriptures well, to chase justice and to love the truth, supporting the well-being and peace for all of us. I look forward to the day when this happens. When it does, I will no longer need these Bible verses as a reminder on my office door.

Anantanand Rambachan

Dear President Biden, Vice President Harris, and Members of the 117th Congress,

The Hindu tradition in which I was raised taught me from a very early age that words have power and are consequential. From my grandparents and parents, I heard, again and again, the story of the Ramayana in which Rama, the prince, went into a homeless exile for fourteen years for the sake of his father's promised word. I memorized the famous words of the text that "one's word must be redeemed, even at the cost of one's life." Fidelity to truth is one of the highest moral obligations of Hindu life, and the sacred teaching that "truth alone triumphs, not untruth," is enshrined in the Veda.

Hindu worship services conclude with an ancient prayer for truth:
>   Lead us from untruth to truth
>   Lead us from darkness to light
>   Lead us from death to immortal life

> " *Fidelity to truth is one of the highest moral obligations of Hindu life …*

The perilous disdain for truth in our public life has led me to see this prayer not only as a supplication to the divine, but as a profound statement about values that are necessary for our flourishing. In the absence of these values, we languish in a death-like darkness and do not prosper in the radiance of light and life. A disregard for truth is never a neutral act. To reject truth is to live in untruth. Truth and untruth are not abstract philosophical concepts, but consequential alternatives that always confront us.

We pray to be led from untruth to truth, because untruth does not nourish goodness and well-being in our individual and social lives. Untruth never serves justice and the common good, since there are always suffering victims, even across generations. Untruth assails us, threatening to normalize and blunt our moral sensibilities into passive resignation. Whenever truth is rejected, it is always because there are interests, personal and corporate, that take precedence over truth. Prominent among these are the greed for power and profit and the false belief that we lift ourselves by crushing others.

"Lead us from untruth to truth" are six profound words that can unite us across our differences. Together, let us renew our commitment to the light of truth that promotes the good life for all and resists the injustice and oppression of untruth.

Dear President Biden, Vice President Harris, and Members of the 117th Congress,

When I turned 18, a Catholic priest, Richard Guastella, sat me down because I was old enough for "the talk" about the sacred obligation of a citizen to vote. Over the years, he became a treasured friend, a cross between an older brother and a first mentor. I followed him into the "family business" by becoming a theological educator. The last time we were physically in each other's company was Inauguration Day 2017. We struggled to make sense of what would become a legacy of "American carnage." His last text message to me stated simply: "No fever but still coughing." He lost consciousness sometime after that. A week later, in the early hours of Holy Thursday 2020, he died from COVID-19 on an ICU ventilator.

> *The long journey toward social friendship after carnage commences with remembering …*

To me, the most haunting words in Pope Francis' October 4, 2020, encyclical, *Fratelli Tutti*, are: "They did not have to die that way." This declaration occurs in reference to the pandemic deaths of the elderly who are too often abandoned in daily life as well as in other crises. These words denounce our all too eager neglect of what the Pope calls "a 'throwaway' world": those deemed most disposable as determined by race, age, disability, socioeconomic status, nation of origin, migrations, documentation. These words indict the needless deaths of migrants at our southern border and of unarmed Black, Brown, and Indigenous lives at the hands of law enforcement. *Fratelli Tutti* was composed from within the lived misery caused by a virus that outed the intersecting and devastating effects of a variety of parasitic social viruses, and countered the anemic, failed, and even violent responses they precipitated.

Pope Francis writes of social friendship; however, such relationships do not begin with the reconciliation of enemies. He reminds us: "It is not possible to proclaim a 'blanket reconciliation' in an effort to bind wounds by decree or to cover injustices in a cloak of oblivion. Who can claim the right to forgive in the name of others?" The long journey toward social friendship after carnage commences with remembering and re-membering those excluded, those pushed to the edges of survival, those whose dignity was demeaned, those violated, those whose blood cries from the ground!

DAY 7, LETTER 7   **Hussein Rashid**

Dear President Biden, Vice President Harris, and Members of the 117th Congress,

As-salaam alaykum wa rahmatullahi wa barakatahu. May God's Peace, Mercy, and Blessings be with you.

In the seventh century, Imam Ali ibn Abu Talib, successor to the Prophet Muhammad's religious and political authority, wrote a letter about good governance. This letter is recognized through history as a model for good leadership. Although it is grounded in a Muslim ethical worldview, it is broadly applicable in practice. One of the points of the letter that I would like to bring to your attention is this line: "A nation in which the rights of the weak are not wrested in an uninhibited manner from the strong will never be blessed."

> " *…when the majority of society is well cared for, society functions well …*

Imam Ali quotes this sentence from Prophet Muhammad as the Imam develops what this teaching means in practice. He says a good leader should pay attention to "the lowest class, those who have no wherewithal, the destitute, the needy, the afflicted, the disabled … Be mindful of God in regard to their rights, for [God] has entrusted these rights to your care." The lesson here is that you need to be most available to those who have no access to you. They are the ones you are entrusted to care for.

The Imam continues to remind us that when the majority of society is well cared for, society functions well, and the elite benefit; but when only the elite are cared for, society falls apart. As Imam Ali says, the elite are not helpful in trials; none are more repelled by justice, nor less grateful.

Following Imam Ali's letter, I implore you to remember those whom we would rather forget. Make them the focus of this administration.

May Allah bless us all.

DAY 8, LETTER 8

Nadia Kizenko

Dear President Biden, Vice President Harris, and Members of the 117th Congress,

The United States consists of citizens not only from different religious traditions, but also of different religious calendars. What was January 6 for most people was December 24 on the Julian calendar. On that day, the "Old Calendarist" Eastern Rite Christians (Russians, Serbs, and others) celebrating Christmas Eve that morning heard Psalm 2: "Why do the nations rage, and the people plot a vain thing?" (v. 1).

Imagine how it then felt to turn on the news and see those very words being played out in the nation's capital. For several hours, none of us knew what would happen. This country, so carefully designed to avoid plots and violent overthrows of government, seemed to be facing such a threat. Some of its citizens, refusing to accept the results of a free and fair election, were attacking the U.S. Capitol itself.

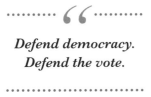

Defend democracy. Defend the vote.

It is not only the last few weeks. The last few months, the last few years, have shown us the lethal force of both plots and rage. Rage and fury and bile spew over social media, unleashing themselves into shattered windows and shuttered streets.

But rage and plots do not come out of nowhere, which brings us back to Psalm 2. The psalm leads with a question. It asks *why* the nations rage and the people plot. In the United States, that question is especially relevant. After all, our democracy was built so that people could express their voices through their votes. Indeed, in Russian, the first language I learned, the word for "voice" (*golos*) is the same word as "vote." But here and now, instead of defending our peaceful voting, some elected officials have urged the people to rage and plot—with fatal consequences.

The lesson is clear. Now that the peaceful transition we prayed for has taken place, your charge is more important than ever. Defend democracy. Defend the vote.

As each of you face the challenge of building a more perfect union, remember January 6 and remember Psalm 2: "Be wise now therefore, O kings: be instructed, O rulers of the earth" (v. 10).

Dear President Biden, Vice President Harris, and Members of the 117th Congress,

I write this letter to you with a heavy and prayerful heart. Our country is not only fiercely divided, but it is now on the precipice of losing the democratic values that have made it a beacon of light to the rest of the world.

We have so many pieces to pick up from the last four years. The scriptures of many of the world's religions preach about the search for Truth, however it may manifest. What has happened, however, is Truth becomes subject to alternative interpretations. We've siloed ourselves in darkness, unable or unwilling to allow the light in.

This moment, like four years ago, prompts me to ask: What can we do to create light together?

Hindu scriptures speak of the role of *dharma*—righteous action for the greater good—in conquering wickedness and evil. There is the story of Prahlad, who remained steadfast in his faith that *dharma*—Vishnu in the form of the lion deity Narasimhan—would conquer even the darkest of forces. Narasimhan killed the evil King Hiranyakashipu as a metaphor of light overcoming the darkness and restoring *dharma*.

> **Hindu scriptures speak of the role of dharma— righteous action for the greater good …**

Today, our *dharma* compels us to rebuild this country. We must be full of faith as we work to ensure that the bonds that have kept this republic together are strengthened through mutual goodwill, pluralism, and respect. But for that to happen, our country needs to trust its political leaders again.

This is why your roles are more important than ever. Whether you supported the previous administration or not, your ability to understand that this country is more than just a sum of political bases will define how we as Americans move forward.

Dharma is about striving for righteousness, even if it comes at a political cost. No seat is worth saving when you have strayed from dharma and denied truth.

I am hopeful that our collective *dharma* will help us to seize the moment to come together and, while acknowledging our differences, work to make this country get back on track towards a more perfect union.

Judith Plaskow

Dear President Biden, Vice President Harris, and Members of the 117th Congress,

At a crucial moment of leadership transition in the history of ancient Israel, the Israelites were about to cross the Jordan River without Moses at their head. As Moses passed on the mantle of authority to Joshua, he enjoined his successor and the assembled community, "Be strong and resolute" (Deuteronomy 31:8). The challenges before the people were multiple and daunting, but Moses urged them not to be afraid or dismayed. His powerful words, which are repeated three times in Deuteronomy 31 (vv. 6, 7, 23), contain a bracing message for the new administration and new Congress as you confront multiple crises facing our divided nation.

Be strong and resolute! Act boldly and decisively to bring the pandemic under control. Do not be afraid to issue a federal mask mandate grounded in the scientific evidence for such an order. Take on as a federal responsibility the production and distribution of adequate PPE for all persons and institutions that so desperately need it. See to the efficient, transparent, and equitable dissemination of the vaccine, prioritizing the needs of those most vulnerable to COVID-19.

> "
>
> *Be strong and resolute!*

Be strong and resolute in addressing the profound social inequities revealed by the pandemic. Ensure that all Americans have access to decent and affordable health care. Pass HR40, which would establish a commission to study and develop reparations proposals so that the country can begin to address the entrenched nature of racial injustice and the prerequisites for systemic change. Acknowledge the ways jails and prisons have been ravaged by the virus and the needs of incarcerated people have been ignored. Respond by passing the People's Justice Guarantee (HR702), which lays out a new vision of criminal justice.

Be strong and resolute in confronting the climate crisis and its relationship to the pandemic. Generously fund scientific efforts to understand the connection between human health and the health of the environment and wildlife populations. Introduce and support legislation to keep oil in the ground and to move toward a sustainable energy future. Commit to surpassing the goals agreed to in the Paris Climate Agreement.

With these and so many other profound challenges facing the nation, now is the time to channel Moses' words and set a transformative agenda with boldness and resolution.

LETTER 9 • *Balaji*: "We must be full of faith as we work to ensure that the bonds that have kept this republic together are strengthened through mutual goodwill, pluralism, and **respect**." **LETTER 12** • *Woodley*: "'Uncle' is a term of endearment and **respect** to wise elders." **LETTER 65** • *Song*: "The 'paradise' Won Buddhists speak of is one founded on treating all people with dignity and **respect** and building a fair and equitable society."

RESPECT

LETTER 18 • *El-Badawi*: "America's standing before the world is regained, not through war and violence, but through the mutual **respect** of its citizens, and citizens from around the world." **LETTER 94** • *Nadella*: "I urge you not to let the morality of your policies and practices be defined by past policies, but by the values of compassion, empathy, and **respect** for everyone." **LETTER 100** • *Fisher-Livne*: "We urge you to build trust, equity, and **respect** for all." **LETTER 87** • *Massingale*: "Without a **respect** for truth and dedication to the truth of the equal sacred dignity and worth of every human being, life together is endangered, compromised, even impossible."

RELIGIOUS VOICES: DAYS 11–20

LETTER 11 | JANUARY 30, 2021

Eboo Patel

Founder and President, Interfaith Youth Core

LETTER 12 | JANUARY 31, 2021

Randy S. Woodley

Distinguished Professor of Faith and Culture and Director of Intercultural and Indigenous Studies, George Fox University and Portland Seminary

LETTER 13 | FEBRUARY 1, 2021

Mitzi J. Smith

J. Davison Philips Professor of New Testament, Columbia Theological Seminary

LETTER 14 | FEBRUARY 2, 2021

Miguel H. Díaz

John Courtney Murray University Chair in Public Service, U.S. Ambassador to the Holy See, Retired, Loyola University Chicago

LETTER 15 | FEBRUARY 3, 2021

Ryan P. Bonfiglio

Assistant Professor, Candler School of Theology at Emory University

LETTER 16 | FEBRUARY 4, 2021

Rachel S. Mikva

Schaalman Professor in Jewish Studies, Senior Fellow, InterReligious Institute at Chicago Theological Seminary

LETTER 17 | FEBRUARY 5, 2021

Kimberly D. Russaw

Assistant Professor of Hebrew Bible, Christian Theological Seminary

LETTER 18 | FEBRUARY 6, 2021

Emran El-Badawi

Program Director and Associate Professor of Middle Eastern Studies, University of Houston

LETTER 19 | FEBRUARY 7, 2021

Corrine Carvalho

Professor of Theology, University of St. Thomas

LETTER 20 | FEBRUARY 8, 2021

Eric D. Barreto

Weyerhaeuser Associate Professor of New Testament, Princeton Theological Seminary

DAY 11, LETTER 11

Eboo Patel

Dear President Biden, Vice President Harris, and Members of the 117th Congress,

We Muslims believe that God created all of us, made us his *abd* and *khalifa* ("servant" and "representative"), gave us responsibility to steward creation, and commands us to do this in the spirit of mercy. One of my favorite lines from the Qur'an reads: "God sent you to be nothing but a special mercy upon all the worlds" (21:107).

Sura 93 from the Qur'an gives even more context on the all-important value of mercy in Islam. The Prophet Muhammad started receiving revelation from God during the month of Ramadan in the year 610. And then suddenly, without warning, the revelation stopped. God had ceased His communication, and the Prophet felt forlorn, bereft.

Then Sura 93 comes crashing through the sky. It opens with God reminding the Prophet that He has by no means abandoned him. God gives him a promise: "What is to come is better for you than what has come before." God also gives him a reminder: "Did He not find you an orphan and take care of you? Did He not find you poor and enrich you?" Then God gives the Prophet a task: "So do not oppress the orphan, and do not drive the beggar away." God ends the sura with this: "And keep recounting the favors of your Lord."

> *… God gives us a central instruction and great responsibility: be merciful.*

This is, in my view, the wisdom of Islam in a few short lines. God is with us, always. What God has done for us is beyond imaginable. We must give to others the gifts that God has given us: support, guidance, sustenance. And we must do so with a spirit of gratitude, because the Source of all things has given us strength.

President Biden and Vice President Harris, your election has given so many of us strength. Please remember that we all come from one God, the Source of all things, and that God gives us great responsibility and a central instruction: be merciful. May your administration live out that command for the good of all God's creatures.

Dear President Biden, Vice President Harris, and Members of the 117th Congress,

I need to begin by saying two things to you, President Biden, that I hope you don't take the wrong way. The first is that I call you "Uncle Joe" when I reference you to friends and family. "Uncle" is not a slur; in our Native American community, "Uncle" is a term of endearment and respect to wise elders. Secondly, I voted for you and fully support you and Vice President Harris, even though Elizabeth Warren and Bernie Sanders were my primary choices. But you should also know that, long before the primary debates, I predicted a Biden/Harris ticket. Why? Because you two are exactly what the country needs right now. I figure if I can set aside my personal bias for the good of the country, others could as well. It seems I was only partially correct.

> *It is your obligation to swiftly mature America by speaking truth in love.*

You face a dilemma and divide even greater than that faced by Abraham Lincoln. At your feet has been laid a climate crisis, a health crisis, including the pandemic, an economic crisis, a racism crisis, a housing crisis, and a crisis in democracy. Ephesians 4:14–15 offers some advice, which we call in our Native American way "speaking from the heart": "Then we will no longer be infants, tossed back and forth by the waves, and blown here and there by every wind of teaching and by the cunning and craftiness of people in their deceitful scheming. Instead, speaking the truth in love, we will grow to become in every respect the mature body … "

It is your obligation to swiftly mature America by speaking truth in love. Truth without love is harsh, and often rejected. Love without truth is not love, but rather neglect, superficiality, and willful indulgence—all of which are the opposite of love. That fine balance of tough love is what we need now for our nation to mature. I learned this the hard way, through having a child addicted to drugs. Time is urgent. Truth and love, President Biden. Grow the country with immediate kindness through relief and support at every level, while speaking the truth to all the past lies, without apology.

Dear President Biden, Vice President Harris, and Members of the 117th Congress,

I am an African American woman and proud resident of the state of Georgia! By now, the first Jewish man, Jon Ossoff, and the first African American man, Raphael Warnock, elected from Georgia to the U.S. Senate have taken their seats in Washington, D.C. In an overwhelmingly white male legislative body, Senators Ossoff and Warnock are among "the least of these."

Representation, representations, and context matter. "The least of these" are contextualized in Matthew 25:44–45: "'Lord, when was it that we saw you hungry or thirsty or a stranger or naked or sick or in prison, and did not take care of you?' Then he will answer them, 'Truly I tell you, just as you did not do it to one of *the least of these*, you did not do it to me.'"

Today, "the least of these" are living in poverty, incarcerated, homeless, sick without adequate health care, and suffocating under oppressive structures. In failing to see and act, we fail Jesus. Matthew 25 convicts our oversight, inaction, and dissonance with God. It summons us to create policies and practices that are commensurate with sightedness and non-victim-blaming compassion and demonstrative of divine values and expectations.

I pray that you establish laws and practices that flaunt our commitment to "the least of these." Commit to a trickle-up agenda rather than exclusionary language. The rhetoric of "the working class" obscures "the least of these" that suffer "daily with their backs against the wall" (Howard Thurman, *Jesus and the Disinherited*). I implore you to consider a living, contextual wage as you continue your efforts to raise the minimum wage. Geography matters. Fifteen dollars an hour is not a living wage everywhere or for everyone.

> " *...establish laws and practices that flaunt our commitment to 'the least of these.'*

Like some of you, I grew up in a "working class" and one-parent household. When my mother's legs failed her, she was no longer "working class." Economically, we were poor. We did not create the poverty we experienced. But when one is poor, it appears one does not deserve quality health care, a living income, decent housing, competent legal representation, or access to quality education. Let us not be ashamed to embrace a radical gospel committed to the elimination of poverty and a just and equal society where "the least of these" flourish.

Dear President Biden, Vice President Harris, and Members of the 117th Congress,

On January 6, the twelfth and final day of Christmas, many Christians celebrate the Feast of Epiphany, which ponders the manifestation of God among us in Christ and in our human stories. The feast originates in the Gospel of Matthew's account of the wise men from the East, sent by King Herod in search of the Christ Child. The wise men followed a rising star until it stopped over the child's house. They entered the house, found the child with his mother Mary, and paid him homage with gifts of gold, frankincense, and myrrh (Matthew 2:9–11).

> *Gift every American with leadership that models our democratic ideals ...*

Matthew's mention of King Herod, a vasal king of the Roman Emperor, signals social-political oppressions at the hand of unjust rulers. Matthew suggests that because Herod felt threatened by Jesus, he ordered the massacre of all infants in Bethlehem (2:16–18). Fearing for Jesus' life, Mary and Joseph took him into Egypt (2:13–15).

Fearing for my own life in 1974, my parents fled Castro's Cuba and migrated to the United States. This personal experience of exile inspired my letter four years ago pleading with the Trump administration to listen to the "huddled masses ... the wretched refuse ... the homeless, tempest-tost." Instead, the Trump administration misused the Bible to justify separating immigrant families, forcing children to live in cages. Such attacks on our nation's religious and civic ideals culminated in the failed attempt by insurrectionists to overturn the results of the free and fair presidential election in the People's House on the Feast of Epiphany.

I take this opportunity as a Cuban exile, concerned citizen, and Catholic theologian who had the honor to serve this country as the ninth U.S. Ambassador to the Holy See to appeal to you to finally enact just and comprehensive immigration reform. This reform must be part of a broader effort to resist what Pope Francis calls the human indifference that plagues our world, which raises physical and relational walls that enslave us within those very walls.

I pray that you follow the rising stars within you to find the missing immigrant children separated from their families. Gift every American with leadership that models our democratic ideals, enables healing, and protects us from all enemies, foreign and domestic.

Dear President Biden, Vice President Harris, and Members of the 117th Congress,

The book of Psalms has nourished the spirituality of Jews and Christians alike throughout the ages. As a collection of honest and poignant prayers, the psalms probe the innermost parts of human experience. From the heights of joy and thanksgiving to the depths of pain and grief, these prayers reflect, as John Calvin once put it, the full anatomy of the soul.

Of particular importance are the psalms of lament. Comprising over 40 percent of the Psalter, these prayers offer heartrending expressions of protest in the face of injustice and tragedy. They begin with piercing interrogatives that underscore that things are not as they should be, such as: "How long must I bear pain in my soul, and have sorrow in my heart all day long?" (Psalm 13:2). Pain pours forth. Shifting from complaint to petition, the psalmist seeks an accounting from the Almighty: "Consider and answer me, O Lord my God! Give light to my eyes, or I will sleep the sleep of death" (Psalm 13:3). Only after sitting with agony and despair for some time—weeks, months, or even years—does the psalmist eventually arrive at words of hope and restoration (Psalm 13:5–6).

As your term begins, there is much to lament in our world: the devastating effects of an ongoing pandemic, families facing unprecedented financial hardships, communities fractured by racial injustice, a nation torn asunder by political strife, natural disasters spurred on by unchecked global warming. At a time like this, I hope the psalms of lament will inspire you to allow space for Americans to give expression to the real pain and grief they are facing. Listen carefully to our laments. Do not respond with superficial optimism that denies the hard realities many are facing. Do not yearn with misdirected nostalgia for a time when things were perceived to be better. Rather, nourish the sort of hope and compassion that can guide us in our present pain.

> "
> *…allow space for Americans to give expression to the real pain and grief they are facing.*

And finally, when you hear words of lament directed at you (and surely you will), do not respond defensively or hostilcly. Remember that words of lament are, at their core, utterances that arise from our common humanity and reflect a type of grief that transcends political boundaries.

Rachel S. Mikva

Dear President Biden, Vice President Harris, and Members of the 117th Congress,

The climate crisis is perhaps the gravest threat we have faced as a nation or species—and the voice of religion has been uneven on this topic. There are courageous calls to confession and action, like in Pope Francis' second encyclical *Laudato Si'* (subtitled "on care for our common home"), but also complacent reassurances that God will not let us destroy the earth.

> *Hope is ... active faith that the world can be different than it is ...*

We can point to centuries-old texts that understood the interconnectedness of all creation, like this 10th-century rabbinic teaching: "The whole world of humans, animals, fish, and birds all depend on one another. All drink the earth's water, breathe the earth's air, and find food in what was created on the earth. All share the same destiny—what happens to one, happens to all" (*Tanna d'bei Eliahu*). Yet we also see scriptural teachings like "Fill the earth and master it" (Genesis 1:28) used to justify exploitation.

There is a particular strength that people of faith can bring in this struggle, however. Our diverse spiritualities cultivate deep roots for hope. The primary messaging strategy for climate action is to show urgency: let's make it better ... or else. But social scientists have demonstrated that if you tell people something must be done or else we are all going to die, most people opt for Door #2. Overwhelming fear leads people to disengage. The prophet Isaiah knew this. He called the Israelites to change their ways in order to avert catastrophe, but instead they yielded to the temptations of fatalism: "Eat and drink, for tomorrow we die" (Isaiah 22:13). When people think, "I can't do anything about it," they succumb to the culture of consumption just as readily as those who pretend it's not happening.

Hope is not idle optimism that all will turn out for the best, but active faith that the world can be different than it is and that we can play a part in shaping it. Aggressively pursuing renewable energy resources, developing carbon capture technologies, expanding desalination and water conservation, changing human diets and lifestyles, seeking economic equity, safeguarding the glorious beauty of our world, teaching simplicity and solidarity, modeling compassion—these are acts of faith. Together, they testify to a collective wisdom that can help humanity change course.

DAY 17, LETTER 17

Kimberly D. Russaw

Dear President Biden, Vice President Harris, and Members of the 117th Congress,

As you settle into your new responsibilities, I encourage you to prioritize the work of rebuilding. While it will be important to designate resources to convert to more efficient energy supplies, update our highways and our energy grid, and invest in the modernization of our public buildings and learning technology, the more difficult building project is much more complicated. On the heels of four years marked by a wholesale attack on policies intended to benefit the most vulnerable among us, the reign of fake news, the squandering of the nation's global reputation, and misinformation regarding a death-dealing pandemic ravaging our communities, we need to undertake an equally urgent building project. Now is the time to rebuild trust in our country.

The good news is you and your team are not the first to take on a critical rebuilding project. In the Bible, Nehemiah returns to lead his community's rebuilding project when he learns his beloved city of Jerusalem is in a state of disrepair. A powerful intentionality exists among the workers who labor alongside Nehemiah to rebuild the wall of Jerusalem. This ancient wall represented trust, stability, and protection for the ancient Israelites—in contrast to a modern-day wall that symbolizes discrimination and intolerance. Although Sanballat and his allies mock this work in the midst of opposition, Nehemiah reports the wall was rebuilt, "for the people had a mind to work" (Nehemiah 4:6).

> *Now is the time to rebuild trust in our country.*

In much the same way the opposition challenged the work of Nehemiah and those dedicated to making Jerusalem a better place to live by rebuilding, so will modern-day naysayers challenge this work of rebuilding trust in the United States of America. There will be cynics and even those who will work to tear down trust as we rebuild it. Be encouraged knowing the people have a mind to work. I ask that you cast a robust and inclusive vision that is undergirded by trustworthiness and provide ways for us to join you in this work. Future generations of Americans cannot afford a prolonged history of distrust.

Emran El-Badawi

Dear President Biden, Vice President Harris, and Members of the 117th Congress,

With this diverse new administration, hope is alive again in America. But our country is bruised and bloodied. In the words of Abraham Lincoln: "a house divided against itself cannot stand." Your predecessor wrought unprecedented hate and harm upon our nation's citizens. We will suffer the consequences of his treason, corruption, proliferation of disease, and rampant racism for years to come.

He was not the first leader to abuse his power or betray his people. Qur'an 27:34 teaches: "Indeed, when kings enter the land, they devastate it. And they make its noblest citizens most humiliated. This is what they do!" It is believed the Queen of Sheba uttered these timeless words of wisdom in protest against the tyranny of King Solomon. These few words contain powerful symbolism and valuable lessons.

First, be not a tyrant before our nation or the world, nor invoke the tyranny of the masses. History will judge many presidents for making war and overthrowing governments across the globe, or for stoking a deadly insurrection here at home. America now sees the cycle of "terror" for what it truly is, projecting the cruelty of white supremacy onto others. Your inauguration speech was the first in American history to address white supremacy, but your condemnation of our nation's greatest scourge is incomplete until you desist from white supremacist wars in the Middle East and elsewhere.

> *... heed the call of women and people of color when they cry out against injustice.*

Second, we recall the stain of American slavery, Jim Crow, and systemic racism, when tyrants humiliated our noblest citizens. But no more! America's standing before the world is regained, not through war and violence, but through the mutual respect of its citizens, and citizens from around the world.

And third, the queen's utterance reminds us to heed the call of women and people of color when they cry out against injustice. They are the ones disproportionately oppressed, and they are our country's greatest source of nobility and progress for the 21st century.

The social and environmental challenges before us are grave and daunting. My hope is that you will ensure that America closes its chapter on terror and tyranny and welcomes a new era where humanity prevails, a world where kindness matters, where diversity and representation matter, where accountability and democracy matter, and where truth and science matter.

Corrine Carvalho

Dear President Biden, Vice President Harris, and Members of the 117th Congress,

I don't envy you. In fact, I admire you that you have taken up this near-impossible task of bringing healing and reconciliation while also leading the nation forward using your own moral compass. It takes courage. It also takes time.

The anger that is tearing apart our nation right now took time to fester, and it springs in large part from fear. As an educator, like First Lady Dr. Jill Biden, I believe the role of education is essential for social transformation. Its aim should not be to teach the right ideology. It should be to teach the ability to think, discern, and join empathy with knowledge.

For my part, as a scholar of the Old Testament who teaches at a Catholic university, I have seen how history continues to repeat itself. I have felt like we are living in the period of Judges when Israel faced multiple challenges and lacked effective leadership. The tragic refrain of the book, which traces how Israelite tribes turned on each other instead of facing their real problems, still rings true: "Everyone did what was right in their own eyes" (Judges 17:6; 21:21). That connection with the past has not been lost on my students this year.

> *... the role of education is essential for social transformation.*

Perhaps the most poignant moment in my classes this past year has been reading the story of Moses, who kills an Egyptian and has to flee because the Hebrew slaves are angry with him (Exodus 2:11–15). I teach in the Twin Cities, where no bystanders assaulted the police officer who killed George Floyd. There was no Moses that day. But my students, who are predominantly white, understood why. They could see how resistance too often brings more trouble to marginalized communities. They suddenly understood systemic racism in action.

So I join Dr. Jill Biden in saying that education is essential for the creation of a new tomorrow. I have hope that with you in office, this will happen, although I am too much of a historian to expect quick change. Is it too late for healing? Like many other Americans, I know we need it.

Eric D. Barreto

Dear President Biden, Vice President Harris, and Members of the 117th Congress,

As you begin your work leading us, let us recognize that these are days of challenge and sorrow. The pandemic has cost too many lives. Racial injustice continues to harm the marginalized. Economic injustice tears at the fabric of our communities. These are terrible and terrifying days for so many.

These are also days of courage and hope. Nurses, support staff, and doctors have healed the sick and comforted the dying. Protestors have called for justice. Millions have voted with love for their neighbors and hope for a better future. These are promising, hopeful days in so many ways.

> *Now, we have called you to a high purpose: to repair what has been broken …*

Now, we have called you to a high purpose: to repair what has been broken; to heal the wounds that have festered in the midst of political neglect; to call us to a unity too long forsaken; to embody a politics in which belonging, justice, and love crowd out fear, self-interest, and the vain pursuit of power.

Of course, you know too well that no politician alone can deliver on such promises. Those politicians who think they can promise what only God can deliver delude themselves and harm the nation. Those politicians who claim only they can solve our problems put themselves on a throne that only God can fill.

The Christian scriptures help us imagine what it might feel like to live in the shadow of God's extravagant grace, to live in a kingdom only God can inaugurate: the end of grief (Revelation 21:4), an answer to creation's groaning for redemption (Romans 8:22), the liberation of the imprisoned (Luke 4:18), blessings to the poor (Matthew 5:3).

So what are we calling you to do? The words of Jesus call us to love our neighbors (Luke 10:27) and to care for those we tend to harm with our neglect (Luke 9:48). To meet this high calling, we all need the help of our neighbors and a force larger than any one politician's ambitions.

So, believe the promises that God has made. Trust that God will accompany you when you make good on our hopes and call you to repair what you have broken when you fall short. In these terrible and promising, terrifying and hopeful days, may you lead us with faith, hope, and love.

LETTER 4 | BRETTLER
"May this administration use scriptures well, to chase justice and to love the truth, supporting the well-being and **peace** for all of us."

LETTER 7 | RASHID
"May God's **Peace**, Mercy, and Blessings be with you."

LETTER 79 | ROSS
"Cultures of **peace** are all around us if we turn our attention to them."

LETTER 25 | HOWARD
"Often justice calls for walking through tension, exposing inequity to establish a positive **peace**."

LETTER 50 | STERN
"May your work create the conditions for wholeness, justice, and **peace** for all in our midst."

P E A C E

RELIGIOUS VOICES: DAYS 21–30

LETTER 21 | FEBRUARY 9, 2021

Karina Martin Hogan

Associate Professor of Theology,
Fordham University

LETTER 26 | FEBRUARY 14, 2021

Mark S. Smith

Helena Professor of Old Testament
Literature and Exegesis, Princeton
Theological Seminary

LETTER 22 | FEBRUARY 10, 2021

Tamara Cohn
Eskenazi

Jacob L. Wright

See titles on page 52

LETTER 27 | FEBRUARY 15, 2021

Tat-siong Benny Liew

Class of 1956 Professor in New Testament
Studies, College of the Holy Cross

LETTER 23 | FEBRUARY 11, 2021

Margaret Aymer

First Presbyterian Church, Shreveport,
D. Thomason Professor of New
Testament, Austin Presbyterian
Theological Seminary

LETTER 28 | FEBRUARY 16, 2021

Paul W. Chilcote

Director, Centre for Global Wesleyan
Theology at Wesley House at Cambridge
University

LETTER 24 | FEBRUARY 12, 2021

Amir Hussain

Chair and Professor of Theological Studies,
Loyola Marymount University

LETTER 29 | FEBRUARY 17, 2021

Matthew L. Skinner

Professor of New Testament,
Luther Seminary

LETTER 25 | FEBRUARY 13, 2021

Lia C. Howard

Student Advising and Wellness Director,
Stavros Niarchos Foundation Paideia
Program, University of Pennsylvania

LETTER 30 | FEBRUARY 18, 2021

Neomi De Anda

Associate Professor of Religious Studies,
University of Dayton

Karina Martin Hogan

Dear President Biden, Vice President Harris, and Members of the 117th Congress,

The Jewish and Christian traditions share the commandment: "You shall love your neighbor as yourself" (Leviticus 19:18; Matthew 22:39). But what does love of one's neighbor actually look like, in the realm of politics? Both traditions hold that it means prioritizing the common good over self-interest. In our current moment in the United States, I submit that loving one's neighbor means prioritizing the common good over individual freedom, as some understand it: the right to make choices that endanger the health and safety of others.

The biblical book of Ruth exemplifies the sacrifice of freedom that love entails. Naomi, who has lost her husband and both of her sons while residing in the land of Moab, is determined to return alone to Bethlehem. She urges her daughters-in-law, Ruth and Orpah, to return to their families; they are free to remarry, to start their lives over again. While Orpah tearfully returns, Ruth "clings to" Naomi (Ruth 1:14). Her declaration of love is well known: "Wherever you go, I will go, and wherever you lodge, I will lodge. Your people will be my people, and your God, my God. Where you die, I will die, and there I will be buried" (Ruth 1:16–17).

> **But what does love of one's neighbor actually look like, in the realm of politics?**

Naomi is silenced by Ruth's refusal to abandon her, but her next words, to the women of Bethlehem, must have pierced Ruth's heart: "Do not call me Naomi, call me Mara ['Bitter'], for the Almighty has made me very bitter. I left here full, but the Lord has returned me empty" (Ruth 1:20–21).

Ruth is able to hear Naomi's words as an expression of grief, not rejection, and she continues to love Naomi "as herself"—that is, as she hopes to be treated. Eventually, Naomi is able to recognize and reciprocate Ruth's love. Naomi comes up with a plan that allows the two of them to form a family with Boaz, a righteous man of Bethlehem.

Many of us can identify with Naomi's bitterness at this moment in American history; but let us follow Ruth's example of steadfast love and work to repair our shattered society by putting the common good first.

Dear President Biden, Vice President Harris, and Members of the 117th Congress,

Recent events in our beloved country have exposed the frailty of much that we have taken for granted. At this time of crisis, we need courageous and creative leadership.

The Jewish Bible (Old Testament) was born in response to catastrophe and defeat. In the face of devastation, some refused to give up hope and set about the task of reimagining what it means to be a people.

In a collaborative effort that is breathtaking in both its scope and creative vision, the biblical authors imagined their separate pasts as one story. They were convinced that their rival communities could join together as one people. In asking what it means to be a people, they rethought every facet of their existence, setting forth a diverse curriculum for a new form of peoplehood.

At its center are laws and statutes demanding love for neighbor and stranger. The intuition guiding this project of peoplehood is that a nation is only as strong as its weakest members. A people that fails to establish an equitable economy cannot endure, let alone be free.

The line emblazoned on our Liberty Bell, "Proclaim liberty throughout the land," comes from the biblical book of Leviticus (25:10). Many Americans consider it a call to *independence*, affirming the privilege of doing as one wishes (as long as it does not harm others). However, its biblical meaning is the opposite: "Proclaim liberty" means recognizing our *interdependence* and creating a socioeconomic safety net that prevents families from falling into irreversible poverty.

At the center of the Torah, and as the foundational text of Judaism, the book of Leviticus teaches that true liberty requires a new infrastructure and society—one that ensures that all, both citizen and stranger, have a secure dwelling place and means of livelihood.

As Americans, we can aspire to nothing less. We call upon you to act, with courage and creativity, to establish this kind of liberty for all. This is a sacred task, and you can count on our support.

Tamara Cohn Eskenazi

The Effie Wise Ochs Professor of Biblical Literature and History, Hebrew Union College – Jewish Institute of Religion

Jacob L. Wright

Associate Professor of Hebrew Bible, Emory University – Candler School of Theology

DAY 23, LETTER 23

Margaret Aymer

Dear President Biden, Vice President Harris, and Members of the 117th Congress,

Popular readings of the story of Zacchaeus the tax collector in the Gospel of Luke portray him as a wealthy and corrupt person who changes because of his faith in Jesus. However, the story that Luke tells is slightly different. In Luke 19, Zacchaeus does not promise to give to the poor or practice reparative justice. Instead, the verbs Luke uses for this story are present tense verbs. While the English translations often read: "I will give to the poor" and "I will pay back," the Greek actually reads: "I do give to the poor" *(tois ptōchois didōmi)* and "I do pay back" *(apodidōdmi)*. This language suggests that Zacchaeus is already doing the work of justice long before Jesus arrives. The people of Jericho think that Zacchaeus is corrupt and sinful, but he is really a man of justice and mercy.

> *... govern our nation following the ways of justice and mercy.*

As you begin your service to the American people, keep your eye out for people like Zacchaeus who have been quietly doing the work of faith and justice for years. Listen to what they have learned about patience, persistence, and grace in the face of enormous pressure. Lean on their wisdom, as you also seek to govern our nation following the ways of justice and mercy.

Cultivate in yourselves deep wells of faith, informed by your many faith traditions, from which you may draw as you seek to serve our nation. Do the work that makes for justice, particularly for "the least of these" (Matthew 25:40), regardless of the polls or popular opinion. May you serve us faithfully.

DAY 24, LETTER 24

Amir Hussain

Dear President Biden, Vice President Harris, and Members of the 117th Congress,

Peace be upon you, and the Mercy and Blessings of God.

I write to you as an American Muslim who is concerned about our country's present and future. For the past four years, we have lived through the Muslim ban, children separated from their parents and put in cages, propaganda given primacy over science, government shutdowns, the normalization of racism and white supremacy, the continued murder of our Black brothers and sisters, a rise in anti-Semitism, disregard for foreign interference in our affairs, nepotism and patronage, and the unnecessary deaths of our people during the pandemic. After all that, we need a return to justice and leadership.

In the Qur'an, we are told directly by the Almighty to stand for justice: "You who have faith, uphold justice and bear witness to God, even if it is against yourselves, your parents, or your close relatives. Whether the person is rich or poor, God can best take care of both. Refrain from following your own desire, so that you can act justly—if you distort or neglect justice, God is fully aware of what you do" (4:135). In our day and age as well, we need to heed these words and come together to work towards a more just society for all of us.

> **With justice, and in faith, we need to right our wrongs and heal our nation.**

The Inauguration called for that same return to justice and unity, and displayed it through speeches, songs, and poems. With the current divisions in our country, I think of our greatest president, Abraham Lincoln. Near the end of the Civil War and less than six weeks before his assassination, President Lincoln concluded his magisterial 1865 second inaugural address with these words: "With malice toward none, with charity for all, with firmness in the right, as God gives us to see the right, let us strive on to finish the work we are in, to bind up the nation's wounds, to care for him who shall have borne the battle, and for his widow and his orphan—to do all which may achieve and cherish a just, and lasting peace, among ourselves, and with all nations."

With justice, and in faith, we need to right our wrongs and heal our nation. I stand ready with other Americans to help with the work ahead of all of us.

DAY 25, LETTER 25

Lia C. Howard

Dear President Biden, Vice President Harris, and Members of the 117th Congress,

Travel with me to a little chapel in Israel built to honor Jesus' Sermon on the Mount. Look up to see stained glass windows depicting the Beatitudes in Latin (the eight blessings recounted by Jesus). My favorite blessing is "*beati pacifici quoniam filii Dei vocabuntur,*" translated as "Blessed are the peacemakers for they will be called children of God" (Matthew 5:9). Each time I read this verse I am challenged anew. Let these words take residence in you the way they reside in glass on those windows. Let them work in your hearts and minds.

> " . . . *peacemaking is the glue needed to piece our country back together in gold.*

We are deeply entrenched in a moment where peacemaking seems like an exhausting upward climb with little reward. How do you remain committed to being a peacemaker when the times you are living in are far from peaceful? The images from the Capitol insurrection haunt me still.

In "Letter from a Birmingham Jail," Rev. Dr. Martin Luther King Jr. expresses his disappointment in "the white moderate . . . who prefers a negative peace which is the absence of tension to a positive peace which is the presence of justice." King challenges us to see that suppressing all tension to create a kind of "peace" is not peace at all. Often justice calls for walking through tension, exposing inequity to establish a positive peace.

Being a peacemaker requires the ability to discern truthfully the areas of conflict between different groups. It calls for accountability and clear-eyed acknowledgment of tensions before groups can be reconciled.

For leaders, there will be temptations to smooth over the cracks in our nation caused by these tensions, to ignore them or cynically exploit them to divide others. I urge you to follow the model of *kintsugi*, the Japanese art form that takes broken pottery and binds the cracks with gold glue. *Kintsugi* teaches us not to forget what broke us as a nation; it shows us that peacemaking is the glue needed to piece our country back together in gold.

May the peacemaking process be gold. May it be beautiful and real, and may we give it lots of attention. May the peace that we feel be a positive peace, the holistic peace of *shalom*. Then, as peacemakers, you will be called children of God.

DAY 26, LETTER 26

Mark S. Smith

Dear President Biden, Vice President Harris, and Members of the 117th Congress,

You are all too aware that we stand at a critically important moment in the life of our country. You have accepted your calling to help move us forward, to embolden our nation to achieve the greater good for our citizens and all who live within our borders. We also know that it is time to face our future with the world. We can do so, burnished with hope in the goodness of creation and humanity fashioned by our Divine Creator (Genesis 1:31) and with courage to do all our work with a standard of justice faithful to that "Judge of all the earth" (Genesis 18:25).

It was this title for God that Abraham used in their conversation over the fate of Sodom and Gomorrah. After a vigorous exchange, God and Abraham arrive at a tipping point of 10 "righteous" persons, which they agree upon as the minimum number for deciding between divine mercy for the innocent and divine justice for the wicked (Genesis 18:32). However, God goes beyond this either/or choice, exercising mercy for the less than 10 innocents and delivering justice for the others. As a nation, our challenge, too, is to find our way to both real justice and real mercy.

> *As a nation, our challenge, too, is to find our way to both real justice and real mercy.*

President Biden, I reserve a word for you as a fellow Roman Catholic. You are trying your best to serve God and the world. We know we were made by our Creator to serve and to love. We are aware of the Church's mostly non-infallible teachings, from which we sometimes must and may in good conscience dissent privately in accordance with Church teaching. We know that it is before God that we ultimately stand. We also know that God knows our hearts and our pains, our struggles and our losses. Yet we also know that we are galvanized by God's exceeding love for us. May you and all who serve in government be galvanized by God's love and by the powerful good of our deepest aspirations for America.

Dear President Biden, Vice President Harris, and Members of the 117th Congress,

"We have always prided ourselves on being not only America the strong and America the free, but America the beautiful," said Lyndon B. Johnson, our 36th president, in a May 22, 1964, speech on the "Great Society." He declared: "Today that beauty is in danger. The water we drink, the food we eat, the very air that we breathe, are threatened with pollution … Green fields and dense forests are disappearing … Today we must act to prevent an ugly America. For once the battle is lost, once our natural splendor is destroyed, it can never be recaptured."

> *… honor God's created nature with its rich biodiversity and care for our common home.*

Long before President Johnson delivered those words, scriptures such as Psalm 104 affirmed the beauty of God's creation and the immense need to care for God's handiwork. In addition to providing water, food, and specific habitats for different creatures—like cedars for birds and high mountains for goats (Psalm 104:17–18)—God created the cycles of day and night to set a rhythm of toil and rest for humans and animals alike (Psalm 104:19–23). We see in this psalm a nonhierarchical and interconnected ecosystem in which a rich biodiversity of life forms is able and enabled to flourish.

The apostle Paul writes in Romans 8:18–27 that creation and humans are all groaning together as they await God's salvation, thus suggesting that the destiny of humanity and of the rest of creation are intimately linked: we flourish and perish together.

The title of Pope Francis' 2015 encyclical captures the ideas of both Psalm 104 and Romans 8. The Latin *Laudato Si'* means "Praise be to You [God]"; the English subtitle reads: "on care for our common home."

More than 50 years after President Johnson sounded that alarm, we are racing against time to reverse the ecological damage. I am encouraged that you have appointed a climate envoy to meet this significant challenge. Given the interconnectedness of the ecosystem, I pray that our country under your administration will be consistent in its policy decisions and practices so that we honor God's created nature with its rich biodiversity and care for our common home.

Dear President Biden, Vice President Harris, and Members of the 117th Congress,

A noble vision will always capture the hearts and minds of Americans, and I believe a truly life-giving vision is dawning. The times in which we live call for a renewed commitment to national unity and peace, decency and truth, racial justice and the well-being of all people. I commend all of you who have cast this kind of vision and deeply desire for all people to live into a future filled with hope.

The prophet Isaiah offers a glimpse of a future shaped by such a noble vision: "The effect of righteousness will be peace and the result of righteousness, quietness and trust forever" (Isaiah 32:17). Jesus brought these images of what he called the Kingdom of God into clear focus in his life and ministry. The Rev. Dr. Martin Luther King Jr. described this divine rule as the "beloved community." Charles Wesley, the great Methodist hymn writer, helps us sing about the "quiet and peaceable reign." I love all these images. What a contrast to the malice and discord of this past era.

> **" I invite you to make this 'beloved community' your central aspiration …**

You have an opportunity to offer a great gift, not only to our nation, but to the world. Just think about what it would mean if your lives and actions in government demonstrated a tireless, unified commitment to the values of justice, peace, unity, and love. What if you, working together toward this grand and alternative vision of life, turned vision into action, leading us forward on such a path. What a legacy you would leave behind!

I invite you to make this "beloved community" your central aspiration and to govern with the sentiments expressed in this prayer hymn of Charles Wesley: "Thy quiet and peaceable reign / In mercy establish below." This reign of *shalom* for which we all yearn points to the gift of reconciliation, the practices of justice and compassion, and the flowering of peace and joy. I pray that, with God's help, you will be the instruments of God's "quiet and peaceable reign" in the living of these days.

DAY 29, LETTER 29

Matthew L. Skinner

Dear President Biden, Vice President Harris, and Members of the 117th Congress,

It's time for leadership that helps Americans tell the truth about our persistent problems. That is harder than it sounds because of all the political pressure to move forward and let the past stay in the past. Yet the desire to "just move on" remains one of our deadliest enemies.

We can learn from the importance that many religions assign to confession. Confession is truth-telling. My Christian tradition understands confession as more than remorse; it acknowledges before God the way things really are. We name and admit the injustices, iniquities, inactions, and indifference for which we are responsible (and from which we suffer), both as individuals and as communities and nations. Authentic confession is not pulling a lever to make God

It's time for confession.

forgive and forget the past. Confessing the truth creates a first step toward changed behavior and repaired relationships. As Christians remember especially today, on Ash Wednesday, confession opens the door to healing (Psalm 51; James 5:16; 1 John 1:9; Mark 1:4–5).

Many American churches and denominations currently find their credibility in jeopardy. It's time for confession. Congregations must sniff out and eradicate the anti-Blackness embedded in our doctrines and traditions. We must insist that anti-immigrant sentiment sickens the body of Christ. We must expose and boldly oppose the tenets of so-called Christian nationalism. A number of Christians need to abandon their dangerous urges to yoke themselves to authoritarian power.

You are politicians; leave that theological reckoning to church leaders. I ask you, as public servants, to lead the wider population by embracing the power of confession. Holding out hope for restoration to come, guide Americans first in laying bare the truths about our nation's ills, especially those crises that are also imperiling our churches.

This can start by ending our culture's unceasing denial of systemic racism and confessing this reality. Acknowledge that conversations about reparations have merit. Hold one another accountable when politicians deploy deceptive or militarized rhetoric. Oppose xenophobia and explain the benefits America has reaped from being a welcoming sanctuary for refugees and other expatriated people.

This country's best days may still be ahead of us. But we will never get close to realizing our great democratic ideals if we refuse to admit our shared history of falling short. It's time.

Dear President Biden, Vice President Harris, and Members of the 117th Congress,

I have seen the sacred ability to dream by so many further shattered over the last four years. To quote Cruz Ramirez in the animated movie *Cars 3*: "Dream small, Cruz … or not at all." For a Latina theologian, dreams devastated by a lack of hope are not new. However, these sorrows only increased as we witnessed at least 23 lives lost and countless others injured during the August 3, 2019, El Paso massacre; the higher impact of the COVID-19 pandemic on people of color; and over 2,805 migrants who lost their lives in pursuit of refuge and safety, like Jamillah Nabunjo.

    Last year, I heard a Latina lawyer working at the Mexico/U.S. border (probably for wages well below what her colleagues make) respond to a group of pastors who asked what changes she would like to see in policies for refugees and migrants. She said: "I would just like to return to where we were before the 'Remain in Mexico Policy' was put into place." For this attorney, a practical commitment to justice meant tightening her vision to a more recent past; she was faced with the need to dream small rather than the ability to dream big.

> **...lead us as a country to live into new dreams with and for each other ...**

    Likewise, I fear that federal leadership will dream small and turn to surface repairs for the deep cracks in our social systems in the U.S. So I write to you today and beg you not to create mere simple remedies for the chaos further awoken over the last four years.

    Instead, lead us as a country to live into new dreams with and for each other, with *the most vulnerable at the core* of the dreaming and the decision-making power. Life is fragile. Multiple communities of people have lived into dreams that attend to the fragility of life. Inspire many generations of leaders from these communities. Use the hundreds of organizations and individuals that have been working together across the Americas to think through social issues, such as *Iniciative Causas Raíz*. Living into big dreams depends on the shared wisdom of many rather than the narrow-sightedness of few.

Letter 1 / Weiss: "Be **HOPEFUL** about your ability to bring about a better world." **Letter 15 / Bonfiglio:** " . . . nourish the sort of **HOPE** and compassion that can guide us in our present pain." **Letter 16 / Mikva:** "**HOPE** is . . . active faith that the world can be different than it is."

Letter 40 / J. Choi: "Do not quench **HOPE** and light scintillating in the visionary's heart." **Letter 41 / Schneider:** " . . . the pandemic has highlighted how the arts and humanities provide a source of comfort, empathy, **HOPE**, community . . ."

Letter 58 / Hayes: "God created the world with both justice and mercy, in the fervent **HOPE** that the world might endure." **Letter 68 / González-Andrieu:** "May you experience incandescent insights, with your eyes fixed on the common good and ready to contribute a spark of **HOPE** to the world."

Letter 93 / Nothwehr: " . . . let us pray with Saint Francis: 'give me true faith, certain **HOPE**, and perfect charity, sense and knowledge'" **Letter 99 / Byron:** "These words of outrage and **HOPE** inspire me to write this open letter."

RELIGIOUS VOICES: DAYS 31–40

LETTER 31 | FEBRUARY 19, 2021

Patrick B. Reyes

Senior Director of Learning Design,
Forum for Theological Exploration

LETTER 32 | FEBRUARY 20, 2021

Stephen Breck Reid

Professor of Christian Scriptures,
George W. Truett Theological Seminary
of Baylor University

LETTER 33 | FEBRUARY 21, 2021

Greg Carey

Professor of New Testament,
Lancaster Theological Seminary

LETTER 34 | FEBRUARY 22, 2021

Shalom E. Holtz

Professor of Bible, Yeshiva University

LETTER 35 | FEBRUARY 23, 2021

Kay Higuera Smith

Professor of Biblical and Religious Studies,
Azusa Pacific University

LETTER 36 | FEBRUARY 24, 2021

Leo Guardado

Assistant Professor of Systematic
Theology, Fordham University

LETTER 37 | FEBRUARY 25, 2021

Yehuda Kurtzer

President, Shalom Hartman Institute of
North America

LETTER 38 | FEBRUARY 26, 2021

Joshua D. Garroway

Sol and Arlene Bronstein Professor of
Judaeo-Christian Studies, Hebrew Union
College – Jewish Institute of Religion, Los
Angeles

LETTER 39 | FEBRUARY 27, 2021

Katherine A. Shaner

Assistant Professor of New Testament,
Wake Forest University, School of Divinity

LETTER 40 | FEBRUARY 28, 2021

Jin Young Choi

Professor of New Testament and Christian
Origins, Colgate Rochester Crozer Divinity
School

Dear President Biden, Vice President Harris, and Members of the 117th Congress,

Remember the child.

Herod murdered children for fear of losing his power (Matthew 2:16–18). Saul destroyed the Amalekites, "child and infant" alike (1 Samuel 15:3–9). Pharaoh murdered all the Hebrew boys (Exodus 1:15–22); and then, with the 10th plague, God killed every first-born (Exodus 12:29–30). Abraham threw out Hagar and Ishmael for Sarah's fear of a shared inheritance (Genesis 21:8–21).

Our religious traditions and our nation are tethered together in the failed imaginations of male leaders who cannot dream big enough dreams for every child. From enslaving Black bodies and committing genocide against Indigenous peoples to limiting access to basic needs like clean water, health care, housing, and education for Black, Indigenous, Latinos/as, recent arrivals, and broader peoples of color, the nation's narrative has been marked by a war on children.

This is not a distant history. On our southern border, children are locked in cages. Five million children in the U.S. live in poverty, 73 percent of whom are children of color. The education gap begins in early education for Latinx, Indigenous, and Black children.

And yet, our tradition also tells us that God met Hagar and Ishmael near the water, called the young boy to live, and spoke great promise over his life (Genesis 21:14–21). Moses' mother placed her infant son in a basket of reeds, and his sister Miriam advocated to Pharaoh's daughter for his mother to care for him (Exodus 2:1–10). Mary saved her child, Jesus, by migrating to a distant land (Matthew 2:19–23).

President Biden,
In the eyes of all children
In the laughter of the child
In full-bellies
In the image of a small pointer finger running across the lines of a children's book
In the hopeful raised arms that calls for us adults to lift and love big hearts
In these moments, you, and this nation, can find its heart and soul.
"Jesus said: 'Let the little children come to me, and do not hinder them, for the kingdom of heaven belongs to such as these'" (Matthew 19:14).
Let all the children come. Let us not hinder them.

Dear President Biden, Vice President Harris, and Members of the 117th Congress,

As you repair the breach of trust and heal the wounds of our community, the Hebrew prophetic traditions encourage you to forgo the talk of scarcity that often accompanies calls for renewal. The biblical story of Elijah in 1 Kings 17 illuminates the challenge before you all.

Elijah ministered during a time of drought and political conflict, so he knew about scarcity. After Elijah announced to King Ahab that God was sending a drought, God sent Elijah to an impoverished widow in Zarephath. "Bring me a little water … Bring me a morsel of food," Elijah said to the widow, who might as well have responded: "You must be kidding." Elijah replied: "Do not be afraid … first make me a little cake of it and bring it to me, and afterwards make something for yourself and your son. For thus says the Lord the God of Israel: 'The jar of meal will not be emptied and the jug of oil will not fail until the day that the Lord sends rain on the earth' " (1 Kings 17:8–16). Elijah had to reassure the widow that her experience of real scarcity, risk, and vulnerability did not subvert the generosity of God. This story reminds us that generosity is key to getting through a drought—or a pandemic.

> *…generosity is key to getting through a drought— or a pandemic.*

Today, wealthy Americans sing songs of scarcity to one another and to middle-class and poor Americans. The lyrics run like this: We do not have enough jobs to allow immigrants. We do not have enough wealth for adequate wages, health care for all, or decent housing. The current pandemic has unmasked disparities that only generosity can assuage.

Mr. President, Madam Vice President, and members of Congress, you must focus on feeding the "least of these" (Matthew 25:45) instead of acquiescing to the self-interest of groups that benefit from and contribute to the broadened disparity in the U.S.

In this time of pandemic and panic that sings a song of scarcity, I encourage you to sing a song of God's promise and generosity that will see us through this drought.

Greg Carey

Dear President Biden, Vice President Harris, and Members of the 117th Congress,

Our nation's profound divisions require an extraordinary quality of leadership. You must discern how to foster healing without compromising the truth. That balance requires wisdom, courage, and magnanimity.

These divisions are especially tragic: not only do they reflect diverse opinions and social experiences, but they are the result of deliberate harm. Like parched twigs on the forest floor, distrust is a fuel primed for combustion. Bad actors have lit the match with devastating results. Now tens of millions of Americans question the legitimacy of our most recent election and therefore of your leadership.

Jesus' teachings encourage us to communicate the truth in straightforward ways. Jesus instructs his disciples: "Let your word be 'Yes, Yes' or 'No, No'" (Matthew 5:37). No wonder, then, that the apostle Paul rejects the premise that he would communicate both yes and no at the same time (2 Corinthians 1:17–20).

Integrity makes its home in simplicity. Nevertheless, wise leaders must discern how to engage people who distort the truth. Jesus models this principle in two conversations. One seeker sincerely asks Jesus: "Good Teacher, what must I do to inherit eternal life?" (Luke 18:18). Jesus rehearses some of the Ten Commandments and then challenges the man to sell all his possessions, give the proceeds to the poor, and follow Jesus. Jesus offered a direct answer; but, unwilling to accept Jesus' invitation, the man departs in sadness.

> *You must discern how to foster healing without compromising the truth.*

Another inquisitor approaches Jesus with the same question; but this man aims to examine Jesus, not to learn from him. Jesus refuses to answer his question directly. First, Jesus asks the man to demonstrate his own grasp of the Torah. Then Jesus tells the famous parable of the Good Samaritan and asks: in the parable, who turns out to be the true neighbor? (Luke 10:25–37). Faced with a person of bad faith, Jesus does not answer questions, he asks them—a strategy he employs in other hostile situations (Luke 20:20–26).

How remarkable that Jesus answers the same question in such different ways. Jesus discerns the difference between honest conversation and bad faith. We citizens rely upon you, our leaders, to tell the truth and build a culture of truth. And we need you all to protect us from deception.

Shalom E. Holtz

Dear President Biden, Vice President Harris, and Members of the 117th Congress,

The book of Deuteronomy constitutes its audience as a family of sorts. For example, it commands the return of lost property as follows (22:1–3): "You must not encounter your fellow's ox or sheep gone astray and ignore them; you must return them to your fellow. If your fellow does not live near you, or you do not know him, you shall take it into your house, and let it be with you until your fellow seeks it and you return it to him. You shall do so for his donkey, and for his clothing, and for any lost object of your fellow's that might go missing from him that you might find. You must not ignore it."

The English words "your fellow" correspond to the Hebrew word that can mean "another member of the biblical community," along with the specific meaning: "your brother." Occurring five times within three verses, this word emphasizes that responsibility towards others stems from a sense of basic kinship. When all involved parties are family, returning missing things becomes much more than an act of common decency.

> *…transform our world from neighborhood into family.*

In a 1954 sermon at Detroit's Second Baptist Church, the Rev. Dr. Martin Luther King Jr. observed: "Through our scientific genius we've made of the world a neighborhood, but through our moral and spiritual genius we've failed to make of it a brotherhood." According to Dr. King, technology had bridged the physical distances between people, but people had not found a way to bridge interpersonal distances between themselves.

Although today we might refer to a more inclusive family, rather than only "brotherhood," we continue to face the same basic problem. At the very same time that computer programs help us solve pandemic-related problems of connecting over physical distances, ideological differences threaten to tear us apart.

The lost-property legislation in Deuteronomy 22 could have been, in Dr. King's terms, a "neighborhood" law, one that ensured nothing more than the return of goods to their rightful owners. Clearly, however, its wording indicates that it means to foster a sense of kinship. It calls all of us, and our leaders most of all, to do what Dr. King thought people had failed to do: to transform our world from neighborhood into family.

Dear President Biden, Vice President Harris, and Members of the 117th Congress,

As you launch a new administration and congressional session, I encourage you to value traditions that a secular democracy can and should share with many religious traditions. One of them, from my own tradition as a Protestant Christian, is that of caring for and honoring the Other—the one who is culturally, racially, or socially different from ourselves.

The story that comes to mind is that of the Good Samaritan in the New Testament Gospel of Luke 10:29–37. The key to the story was that the Samaritan was a social-cultural Other. He represented a tradition that the Jews opposed. To put it another way, in my reading of this passage, he represented what the Insider Group considered to be problematic and therefore a danger to their own identity. Jesus told his followers that this Samaritan acted in a way to be honored and emulated.

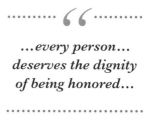

…every person… deserves the dignity of being honored…

This story teaches that every person, even from a religious group different from my own, deserves the dignity of being honored as I want to be honored, that they share with me the same standards of behavior that put others first, and that they likely have something important to teach me.

As a scholar teaching at an evangelical institution, I have been saddened by how many white people representing this tradition have ignored this story and these important lessons. We honor Rev. Dr. Martin Luther King Jr. for his espousal of nonviolence, but then we find ways to justify our own violent acts against the Other, ignoring their dignity and humanity. This should not be. If we espouse nonviolence only for Black people but insist on violence when white people feel threatened, then we have ignored our own scriptures. Moreover, we have ignored the values of a healthy and robust democracy.

May you receive a blessing as you seek to enact, in legislation and in policy, the spirit of the Good Samaritan and similar lessons from all religious traditions.

Leo Guardado

Dear President Biden, Vice President Harris, and Members of the 117th Congress,

Is it a crime for people of color to seek life? I was nine years old in 1991 when my mother and I crossed the border into the U.S., fleeing violence in El Salvador from a war funded by the United States. Had we asked for asylum at the border, we would have been returned like the thousands of other Central Americans that the U.S. government was sending back to possible death. I can write this letter now because we crossed the line and lie of criminality like so many who continue to cross it today.

Is it a crime to provide border crossers with humanitarian aid? In Southern Arizona, volunteers with organizations like No More Deaths/No Más Muertes and Samaritans are regularly harassed and targeted by Border Patrol for providing border crossers with life-saving water, food, and medical assistance in the desert. They exercise a true and holy humanity at the risk of arrest and incarceration.

Is it criminal to protect persecuted communities from ICE? Across the country, ICE terrorizes communities of color, forcibly separating families. Houses of worship, out of their faith convictions, provide sanctuary for days or years to persons threatened with deportation. They uphold the fundamental principle that persons who fear returning to their place of origin must be afforded some means of protection.

> " . . . *loose the bonds of injustice* . . .

As you begin the holy work of healing the festering wounds of this nation and—in the words of President Biden's inaugural address—responding to the "cry for racial justice some 400 years in the making," let us not forget that legislation surrounding migration has served and continues to serve as a tool of racism and the myth of white supremacy. Decriminalizing migration and providing aid and protection to save lives are essential steps in healing the social and moral wounds of this nation. To use the words of the prophet Isaiah, which are as relevant now for this country as they were in his time: "…loose the bonds of injustice…undo the thongs of the yoke…let the oppressed go free… break every yoke… Then your light shall break forth like the dawn, and your healing shall spring up quickly" (Isaiah 58:6, 8).

Dear President Biden, Vice President Harris, and Members of the 117th Congress,

Please ask more of us.

The challenges facing our divided country right now are immense, and you display great courage in seeking public office to address them. I know that for many of you, this work is an act of service.

It is commonplace to think as government principally as "for the people." But in the rabbinic tradition, citizenship is understood as a framework for individuals to take responsibility for the welfare of their society. The Mishnah, an early third-century book of law, defines for us that either long-term residency or property ownership creates a sense of belonging to the town. According to Tractate Bava Batra 1:5, residents of a town may compel their neighbors to contribute to the building of a gate-house for the settlement and a door to the courtyard.

> *Good citizenship is rooted in obligation.*

This rabbinic vision of citizenship is rooted in service to the common good. The Mishnah is not aware of a language of "rights" that are bestowed by the society on citizens except those benefits earned through collective responsibility. If all of us pay for the town to have a proper gate, we gain security; if all of us maintain the upkeep of the courtyard doors, we have privacy. As Robert Cover wrote, Judaism's language of obligations as the glue of a healthy society stands in contrast to America's fixation on rights.

Even as we love and cherish our rights, we Americans are losing our grasp on the covenantal relationship between rights and obligations. At pivotal moments in American history in the past, when our country faced extraordinary crises, our greatest leaders turned to us and made demands. Even as it was their responsibility to provide for our physical safety and our economic well-being, they also understood that great leadership requires creating cultures of collective responsibility for the greater good.

So I implore you to remind us of our obligations. Our society will only repair itself when we as its citizens participate collectively in that work. I hope you will not just ask what you can do for us, but start asking us what we can do for our fellow Americans. Good citizenship is rooted in obligation. We are ready to step up.

Joshua D. Garroway

Dear President Biden, Vice President Harris, and Members of the 117th Congress,

Almost 800 years ago, a small community of German Jews faced a problem. Their town barely had a minyan, the 10 adults required for communal prayer. When major holidays came around, and a townsperson or two celebrated with family in another city, the town struggled to muster 10 men for its own festival observance. So the townspeople wondered: does Judaism allow the community to compel a person to remain in town to make a minyan?

This question was put to Germany's leading rabbi at the time, Meir of Rothenburg (1215–1293). He argued that the community does have such power because communal prayer constitutes a *tzorech gadol*, a great need. He noted that Jewish law similarly permits a town to force the baker to keep the bakery open on the eve of a festival so that residents have fresh bread for their celebrations. Sometimes, the needs of the community prevail over individual liberty. The rabbi added a caveat, however: if a town has 11 Jews, not 10, it may not prevent a person from leaving out of fear that one of the remaining 10 might fall ill and deplete the quorum. Having the extra person available to make the minyan is helpful, but not essential. Coercion may at times restrict liberty, in other words, but only when it is absolutely necessary.

> *…use the coercive power of the state cautiously…*

While the struggles of a medieval town might seem remote from the concerns of a modern nation of more than a quarter-billion citizens, the basic tension between communal need and individual freedom rests at the heart of a country whose Constitution aims to "promote the general welfare" but also to "secure the Blessings of Liberty." Many Americans fear that the balance in recent years has tilted toward the state and that liberty has been unduly compromised by the government's power to tax, to police and incarcerate, to regulate business and trade, and so on. The restrictions resulting from the pandemic have exacerbated these concerns.

As we look ahead to the scourge lifting and normalcy returning, I urge you to consider the wisdom of Rabbi Meir: use the coercive power of the state cautiously to meet the great needs of the public, while ever safeguarding our inalienable and divinely endowed right to be free.

Katherine A. Shaner

Dear President Biden, Vice President Harris, and Members of the 117th Congress,

The #BlackLivesMatter protests from the summer of 2020 and a white supremacist insurrection in January 2021 should not be equated. The two are morally, ethically, and spiritually incomparable.

Deadly, systemic racism devalues African American citizens and other people of color in our country. Such racism implicitly and explicitly advocates violence, exploitation, and neglect. #BlackLivesMatter demands reparation for these historic wrongs. White supremacists, in contrast, seek homogeneity and believe power should be concentrated in one race, religion, and set of social values—a logic that values white lives more than others.

Jesus' disturbance in the temple (Mark 11:15–19) helps illustrate this logic. In this story, Jesus enters the Jerusalem temple and, in a fit of righteous anger, overturns the money changers' tables and creates chaos among merchants. Jesus' actions attract the attention of the authorities, who plot his death. Americans love to tell this story as an allegory of how righteous anger fuels the political agenda of charismatic leaders across the political spectrum.

> *The same communal ethic must drive American politics…*

This story can paint anger as a productive tool of justice. Yet, one charismatic man—even one called Lord and Savior, Son of God—does not single-handedly change the course of justice with his disruption. The incident in Mark could not, would not, and did not happen without the organization and cooperation of enslaved people who operated the money changers' tables. Or the impoverished women selling small animals to religious pilgrims. Or the disenfranchised workers earning precarious wages. These enslaved people, women, and workers knew how to stage Jesus' protest—a protest that was not about takeover, but about unshackling people from state-sanctioned violence and exploitation. Mark 11:18 notes that after the protest, a crowd listened, spellbound, to Jesus' teachings. Then the movement must have continued working toward emancipation for the sake of the liberative, equitable community God plans for our world. Had they not continued organizing, we would not know the hope of justice, liberty, and equity today.

The same communal ethic must drive American politics: no one, not even Jesus, enacts liberty, equity, or justice without first building community across difference. Build that community. Empower those who already have.

Jin Young Choi

Dear President Biden, Vice President Harris, and Members of the 117th Congress,

As an immigrant, I am concerned with U.S. immigration and foreign policies. The U.S. wars in Afghanistan and Iraq started under the Bush administration, and the former is still ongoing. Trump's discriminatory executive orders have indelibly impacted refugees, immigrants, members of LGBTQ communities, and more.

However, President Biden, your State Department speech demonstrates your determination to restore diplomacy in U.S. foreign policy, as well as to bolster democracy by defending equal rights of all people. I applaud your effort to open the door to refugees worldwide. You state that "we shined the light of…liberty on oppressed people." U.S. moral leadership can use its global power to promote liberation and peace and serve as an example for the world.

> **Do not quench hope and light scintillating in the visionary's heart.**

We can find inspiration for such a global vision in Jewish and Christian scriptures. Isaiah proclaims God's message: "I have given you as…a light to the nations" (42:6). Note that these words were given to a people in exile, not to a powerful empire. Just as the prophet Jeremiah feels called by God to fulfill a mission (1:5), Paul understands himself called to proclaim the good news of Christ among nations under Roman imperial rule (Galatians 1:15–16).

United States global leadership will never shine via white supremacist liberalism and imperial exceptionalism. Instead, as the poet Amanda Gorman envisioned, the future of U.S. democracy should not be based on the inherited pride of being American, but on shared power. This young Black poet dares to climb the hill built not on "the blade," but on "all the bridges we've made." Inspired by Micah 4:3–4, she anticipates the "promised glade" where "everyone shall sit under their own vine and fig tree and no one shall make them afraid."

I hear this message not only as a biblical scholar, but also as a transnational subject living with transmitted memories and traumas of the unfinished Korean War. Sadly, such U.S.-involved or -backed wars continue. Work with the international community on peace processes to end wars and occupations and cut military spending. Do not quench hope and light scintillating in the visionary's heart.

LETTER 29 | SKINNER

"It's time for leadership that helps Americans tell the **truth** about our persistent problems."

LETTER 85 | CHAPPLE

"Mahatma Gandhi employed two core precepts of Yoga to free India from British colonial rule: nonviolence (*ahimsa*) and holding always to **truth** (*satyagraha*)."

LETTER 63 | SHEPPARD

"We need your prophetic leadership and vision of justice, inclusivity, **truth**, and hope for the future of the United States."

LETTER 58 | HAYES

"Justice, grounded in **truth**, makes social relationships possible through a commitment to what is fair and right."

LETTER 3 | BOWENS

"Do we speak out against hate, do justice in an anti-justice world, proclaim **truth** in a world that craves fantasy?"

LETTER 95 | DOUGLAS

"It is past time that the U.S. confronts the **truth** that American exceptionalism— the deeply rooted social construct to protect whiteness at all costs— depends on a fundamental narrative of anti-Blackness."

RELIGIOUS VOICES: DAYS 41–50

LETTER 41 | MARCH 1, 2021

Tammi J. Schneider

Danforth Chair in Religion, Claremont Graduate University

LETTER 42 | MARCH 2, 2021

Karoline M. Lewis

Marbury E. Anderson Chair in Biblical Preaching, Luther Seminary

LETTER 43 | MARCH 3, 2021

Jennifer L. Koosed

Professor of Religious Studies, Albright College

LETTER 44 | MARCH 4, 2021

Shawnee M. Daniels-Sykes

Professor of Theology and Ethics, Mount Mary University

LETTER 45 | MARCH 5, 2021

Jacqueline M. Hidalgo

Professor of Latina/o/x Studies and Religion, Williams College

LETTER 46 | MARCH 6, 2021

Serene Jones

President, Union Theological Seminary

LETTER 47 | MARCH 7, 2021

Ki Joo (KC) Choi

Professor of Theological Ethics and Chair of the Department of Religion, Seton Hall University

LETTER 48 | MARCH 8, 2021

Jean-Pierre M. Ruiz

Associate Professor of Theology and Religious Studies, St. John's University, New York

LETTER 49 | MARCH 9, 2021

Matthew Kraus

Associate Professor of Judaic Studies, University of Cincinnati

LETTER 50 | MARCH 10, 2021

Elsie R. Stern

Vice President for Academic Affairs, Associate Professor of Bible, Reconstructionist Rabbinical College

Dear President Biden, Vice President Harris, and Members of the 117th Congress,

In light of the host of issues facing our country—including COVID-19, lost jobs, failing infrastructure, climate change, institutionalized racism, unjust immigration policies—it is easy to forget what sustains so many of us: the arts and humanities. When I wrote a letter to the previous administration in 2017, the National Endowment for the Arts and National Endowment for the Humanities were being threatened with extinction. While that is no longer the case, the pandemic has highlighted how the arts and humanities provide a source of comfort, empathy, hope, community, and—what we so badly need right now—joy.

> *…the arts and humanities provide a source of comfort, empathy, hope…*

    The Hebrew Bible helps us appreciate the longstanding importance of the arts and humanities, especially music and poetry. In Genesis 4:21, Jubal is named the ancestor of all who play the lyre and the pipe. Later, David—who is regarded as the legendary author of the book of Psalms— soothes King Saul's terrors with the lyre (I Samuel 16:23). In these days of isolation during the pandemic, orchestras, choirs, and school bands have found ways to produce music on Zoom to comfort the world.

    In the book of Exodus, after the Israelites miraculously cross the sea, the prophet Miriam and the women go out with hand drums, singing, and dancing to celebrate their liberation from Egypt (Exodus 15:20–21). In the book of Judges, Deborah, the legendary judge and prophet, leads Israel into battle and then sings of Israel's victory ushering in a period of peace (Judges 4–5). These and other biblical citations (like 1 Samuel 18:6–7) testify to the celebrated role female performers played in ancient Israel as they elevated momentous occasions with music, song, and dance.

    On Inauguration Day, we saw a young woman play this precise role. In the words of Amanda Gorman, our country's new national treasure and National Youth Poet Laureate, please maintain the arts and humanities so that:

> "We will not march back to what was,
> but move to what shall be.
> A country that is bruised but whole,
> benevolent but bold,
> fierce and free."

Dear President Biden, Vice President Harris, and Members of the 117th Congress,

I truly never imagined that in my lifetime I would see a woman in the role of president or vice president of the United States of America. This pessimism was not due to absence of hope, but an awareness that misogyny and patriarchy still thwart ideals for public and political leadership. I pray that this national milestone is not mistaken for problems solved.

In the church, I have witnessed all too often the election of women to prominent leadership roles, which then occasions complacency in the work toward dismantling the sin of systemic sexism. In doing so, the church has sidelined the biblical and theological commands that demand persistence and vigilance in advocating for the full glory of the reign of God.

Jesus knew well the human tendency to circumvent the capacity of God's love. In the Gospel of John, as Jesus sets out to travel from Jerusalem to Galilee, he takes his followers through Samaria. Outside of the Samaritan town of Sychar, Jesus encounters a Samaritan woman at a well. It wasn't necessary to go through Samaria geographically. But it was necessary theologically: necessary for the disciples to realize what "for God so loved the world" really looks like (John 3:16). Jesus loves this unnamed Samaritan woman, and Jesus needs her. Jesus' mission will not be complete without her embodying this divine love. From the testimony of this unlikely "disciple," her townspeople learn that a new rule is afoot. God's reign will only be realized with her witness. But the disciples resist, as do we: how could Jesus be talking to a woman?

> *…misogyny and patriarchy still thwart ideals for public and political leadership.*

The frequent temptation of the church is to bask in its successes so as to skirt its responsibilities—dodging the truth about itself and assuming an inherent holiness. I see parallel presuppositions in our nation. We are tempted to rest on our laurels and conclude that a vision for democracy is democracy achieved, or that a woman one step away from the presidency is sexism and misogyny overcome.

I pray that you will fully embrace and embody this historic moment—a moment that will unleash both resistance and self-righteousness, but also a moment when the fullness of democracy's dreams has never been closer.

Jennifer L. Koosed

Dear President Biden, Vice President Harris, and Members of the 117th Congress,

Reproductive justice is not a concept found in Scripture. Yet the basic tenets of reproductive justice—the ability to decide if and when to have children, access to the information and technologies needed to actualize that decision, medical care for healthy pregnancies and births, the material support necessary to raise a family—are grounded in principles that are deeply biblical and profoundly religious.

> " *...reproductive justice is a matter of religious freedom...*

In Judaism, the most fundamental of these principles is *k'vod habriot*, human dignity. Derived from the declaration that all people are created "in the image of God" (Genesis 1:27) and the idea that God's own *kavod* ("glory") fills the earth (Isaiah 6:3), the principle of human dignity is far-reaching and can take precedence over other biblical mandates. Bodily autonomy is central to human dignity. An embryo grows inside our innermost being; a fetus lodges right under our heart. To use our bodies to spark and grow life is powerful; to force a body to do so is a perversion of the divine image.

Human dignity also entails provision and protection. The Bible is deeply concerned with providing what parents need to raise healthy, happy, and strong children. After Hagar and her son are driven out of their home and the boy nearly dies from lack of water, in the depths of her despair, Hagar cries out. God hears, God responds, and God saves Hagar and her son (Genesis 21:14–21). From this and other biblical stories. we learn that reproductive justice means caring for our children: providing the clean water, abundant food, safe housing, and quality education that children need to thrive.

In my 2017 letter to the last administration, I argued that reproductive justice is a matter of religious freedom, and true freedom of religion means allowing different people to make different decisions in conversation with their own religious traditions. The government can and should provide access to medical care and build an infrastructure of support for families. Such governmental actions empower people to make their own decisions about what happens in and to their bodies. But government interference in more intimate matters violates the Constitution; even more, such interference violates human dignity and the glory of God.

Shawnee M. Daniels-Sykes

Dear President Biden, Vice President Harris, and Members of the 117th Congress,

The Hippocratic Oath recited by all physicians contains the phrase *primum non nocere*, "First, do no harm." This pledge is rooted in both faith and reason, calling human beings to acknowledge that all human life is fragile and must be handled with special care and attention. God created each human person of incomparable worth, with equal potential to flourish with dignity (Genesis 1:27–28).

During the last four years under the administration of Donald J. Trump, many tragic harms were committed that were an affront to human dignity and prevented human flourishing. Following the definition of Sister Joan Chittister, OSB, I contend that our prior president may have been pro-birth, but he was not pro-life. Sister Chittister explains: "I do not believe that just because you're opposed to abortion, that that makes you pro-life. In fact, I think in many cases, your morality is deeply lacking if all you want is a child born, but not fed, not a child educated, not a child housed. And why would I think that you don't? Because you don't want any tax money to go there. That's not pro-life. That's pro-birth. We need a much broader conversation on what the morality of pro-life is."

> **God created each human person of incomparable worth…**

As you enter into your work as elected public servants—official representatives of the highest offices in the United States government—my hope is that in every decision you make, you will ask: who might be harmed, marginalized, or killed by this decision? My prayer is that you will discuss among yourselves how your decisions might bring about a more beatific vision on Earth, as it is in Heaven, where all people flourish through the praise, reverence, and support of God, self, and neighbor.

Dear President Biden, Vice President Harris, and Members of the 117th Congress,

I am exhausted. Four years ago, I wrote of the absence of hope and of how only determination remained: the determination to build a more socially, racially, and economically just United States of America, no matter the odds. Four years later, that determination has been strained. As for so many, this past year of the pandemic exacerbated my weariness, leaving me overwhelmed by the losses of at least half a million in the U.S. alone, more loved ones than we can truly count. Every day I crave an end to so many struggles, and every day *la lucha* ("the struggle") continues.

> " *…I permit my exhausted determination the smallest of hopes…*

I am one of the privileged in the pandemic—safely employed, fed, warm—so my exhaustion is small. I also know my cries of exhaustion may feel pressing now, but they have a long history, uttered by countless others with far greater cause. In 1964, civil rights leader Fannie Lou Hamer famously stated: "I am sick and tired of being sick and tired." In 1983, Chicana author Gloria Anzaldúa wrote: "Perhaps like me you are tired of suffering and talking about suffering." Even that enigmatic book of Revelation, which offers no direct words of hope, underscores the quest for "patient endurance" in three of its seven opening letters.

Witnesses to persistence, Hamer, Anzaldúa, and Revelation share an unflinching account of dominant society's violence alongside formidable visions of transformation. I learned from them that persistence requires a realistic accounting of what has been done even as we dream a future that cannot, must not, look like the past.

As this new day brings a new *lucha*, I permit my exhausted determination the smallest of hopes that, in Amanda Gorman's moving words, we aren't "broken but simply unfinished." I also hope that we now take the time to mourn our dead, to truly reckon with the violence we have wrought on each other, and that we refuse any fantasy of a better past. Anzaldúa once wrote: "There are no bridges, one builds them as one walks!" As we walk, may we build a bridge to a future that reckons with the past but refuses to resemble it.

Dear President Biden, Vice President Harris, and Members of the 117th Congress,

You have been elected to lead us during one of the most traumatic times in our history. Right now, we are a quaking, fearful country. Violence and death have drawn so near that their horror has made their home in our bones.

> *We need your calming, feeding, healing actions at this moment in time …*

In my own Christian tradition, the Road to Emmaus story comes to mind (Luke 24:13–35). Jesus' disciples have just gone through a devastating crisis. Their beloved leader is gone, they are riddled with fear and anxiety, and they are compulsively recounting "all that has happened" to them. Our whole nation is trapped in that same panicked chatter about "all that has happened."

A stranger starts walking beside Jesus' disciples, listening to trauma spilling out of them. They aren't sure what to make of the stranger, but he doesn't leave. He just keeps walking. When night falls, they invite him to their campfire dinner.

Something unexpected happens. The stranger takes their fire-cooked food and serves them. They suddenly recognize—through the work of his hands, his actions—that the stranger is Jesus. Their trauma is calmed and their overwhelming fear and distrust starts to ebb. Maybe they laugh for the first time in a long time.

What I love about this story is that during the meal, they keep forgetting who he is. The trauma inside them keeps popping back up, and they need reminding, calming and feeding, over and over again.

I lift up this story because it reminds us that people who are afraid and suffering can easily lose track of reality. Trauma does that. It also tells us that the way to calm harmed souls is not through words alone but through actions: feeding hungry bodies, mending harms, holding fear rather than being afraid of it.

We need your calming, feeding, healing actions at this moment in time more than we need anything else. Love us, Mr. President, Madam Vice President, and members of Congress. Try to love us all, as we stumble along our many Emmaus Roads. And don't give up when we forget. Feed us, the people.

Dear President Biden, Vice President Harris, and Members of the 117th Congress,

Since the inauguration, I've been reflecting on 1 Corinthians 12:20–23: "As it is, there are many members, yet one body. The eye cannot say to the hand, 'I have no need of you' … On the contrary, the members of the body that seem to be weaker are indispensable, and those members of the body that we think less honorable we clothe with greater honor." Why these verses?

There's been so much talk lately of the decline of American democracy, and there are good reasons for this worry. You don't need me to remind you that the racism, xenophobia, anti-Semitism, and authoritarian rhetoric that have been amplified by the previous administration—and distilled to their logical conclusion on January 6—have revealed an inconvenient truth about the health of our republic.

We have a chance to change this narrative around, but only if you'll lead us to recover a sense of what it takes to be a democracy. We've been focused, understandably, on the sacredness of voting and the rule of law. But even voting and the rule of law will inevitably devolve into yet additional tools for hyperpartisan exertions of power and exclusion unless we are willing to *first* see each other as legitimate partners in the democratic enterprise. This doesn't mean that every grievance and belief that we might hold are meritorious, but it does mean that we must strive to better understand each other's fears, concerns, and pains. This is a commitment that has, sadly, fallen out of fashion.

> " *Democracy only works if its members are willing to be for one another …*

Democracy only works if its members are willing to be *for* one another, regardless of party affiliation. For Christians, this proposition should hardly sound novel—we need only to recall the verses that began this letter. Nevertheless, it is a difficult and uncomfortable proposition. The moral habit of being for one another, even with those with whom we disagree vehemently, is the very precondition for bipartisanship, which has eluded our democracy for too long. My hope is that you will show us how to relearn this demanding moral habit. This is an education that we desperately need if we want our democracy to flourish.

Dear President Biden, Vice President Harris, and Members of the 117th Congress,

When I try to convince my students that the Bible should be familiar to them no matter their religious affiliation, images do the job more persuasively than any arguments I might advance. These images include a photo of Inauguration Day, when the incoming President of the United States takes the oath of office with a hand resting on the Bible. Other images are troubling, among them the 45th president of the United States standing in front of St. John's Church holding a copy of the Bible on June 1, 2020, after he used tear gas and rubber bullets to disperse a peaceful crowd protesting the murder of George Floyd. The unsettling images also include a rioter outside the Capitol on January 6, 2021, holding up a Bible as though it were body armor, and people wielding posters with citations from the Bible as though they were weapons.

> *May this be a time when the words of our sacred texts move us to change the world ...*

It matters much less what we do with the Bible itself than what we do with its words once we open it! Author Václav Havel received the 1989 Peace Prize of the German Booksellers' Association for his role in the "Velvet Revolution," which brought a peaceful end to Communist rule in Czechoslovakia. Havel's acceptance speech invoked the Bible: "In the beginning was the Word; so it states on the first page of one of the most important books known to us. What is meant in that book is that the Word of God is the source of all creation ... If the Word of God is the source of God's entire creation then that part of God's creation which is the human race exists as such only thanks to another of God's miracles—the miracle of human speech." Havel went on to ask: "Is the human word truly powerful enough to change the world and influence history?"

The answer to this question is an unequivocal yes. We have witnessed the power of words—even words from the Bible—to cause enormous harm. Yet, if we take Havel's reflections on the Prologue of John's Gospel seriously, words also have the power to bring about tremendous good. May this be a time when the words of our sacred texts move us to change the world, inspiring us to work to make a real difference for the common good.

Dear President Biden, Vice President Harris, and Members of the 117th Congress,

After the Israelites suffered the great trauma of Jerusalem being attacked, the Temple destroyed, and our people exiled, the final books of the Hebrew Bible provided empathy, comfort, and a roadmap to restoration. Then and now, returning and rebuilding from exile is no easy task.

We have suffered together in exile: "By the waters of Babylon we laid down and wept as we remembered Zion" (Psalm 137:1).

We look to you to return us from exile: "Thus said Cyrus, ruler of Persia: '…let any one of you go back to Jerusalem'" (Ezra 1:2–3).

We look to you to rebuild: Cyrus "shall say of Jerusalem: 'She shall be rebuilt,' and to the Temple: 'You shall be founded again'" (Isaiah 44:28).

We will join you and return together: The "people came up from the captive exiles…who returned to Jerusalem and Judah" (Ezra 2:1).

We will join you and rebuild together: "We, God's servants, will start building" (Nehemiah 2:20).

We pledge to care for those not prepared to return from exile: "All who stay behind…let the people of their place assist them" (Ezra 1:4).

And we mourn those who did not survive the exile: But "the memory of the righteous shall be for a blessing" (Proverbs 10:7).

We recognize that not all support rebuilding: "Thereupon the people of the land undermined the resolve of the Judeans and made them afraid to build" (Ezra 4:5).

Yet we are responsible to build for everyone: "For My House shall be called a house of prayer for all peoples" (Isaiah 56:7).

We look to renew, to rebuild. Our materials are a vision of a better future and the memory of past pain and blessings: "Let us come back; renew our days as of old" (Lamentations 5:21).

There is memory. There is suffering. There is loss. Exile has been prolonged.

And yet together we can transform the shared experience of exile into the rebuilt foundations of that better future: "All the people raised a great shout extolling God because the foundation of the House of God had been laid" (Ezra 3:11).

We entered exile in sorrow. Let us return and rebuild in joy as a new and better people.

Elsie R. Stern

Dear President Biden, Vice President Harris, and Members of the 117th Congress,

I write on the fiftieth day of your administration—the midpoint of your first 100 days.

In Jewish time, we are also "in the thick of it." We are in the middle of the Jewish calendar and about halfway between the holidays of Purim and Passover. In our annual cycle of scripture readings, we are almost halfway through the Torah (Genesis through Deuteronomy). Each of these middle moments has its own character and its own message.

In the Hebrew calendar, we are in the month of Adar, about which we are advised to increase joy. In the middle moments, the euphoria of a new start wanes, and we need to work harder to maintain buoyancy, optimism, and vision. At the same time, we are halfway between Purim and Passover. On Purim, we read the book of Esther, which reminded us of the danger of chaos and misrule. On Passover, we will celebrate the possibility of liberation. In this space in between, the fear and relief of Purim linger even as we begin to anticipate the liberation to come.

> *This is an 'all hands on deck' project …*

This week we are also nearing the middle of the Torah, as we finish the account of the building of the tabernacle in the book of Exodus. This is an "all hands on deck" project whose results are palpably transformative: "When Moses finished the work … the Presence of God filled the tabernacle" (Exodus 40:34). The completion of the tabernacle makes a place for the holy amidst the nation. Next week, we will begin reading Leviticus—a policy and procedures manual for the ancient priests. Thus this juncture in the Torah reminds us that both the adrenaline-fueled act of building and the ongoing efforts of governing (be it temple or nation) are sacred work.

In this moment in the middle, may you find energy and joy as you lead us, we hope, from chaos to liberation, past the highs of the "start-up" phase into the sustained work of governing. May your work create the conditions for wholeness, justice, and peace for all in our midst.

★ **LETTER 2 (S. SINGH):** *". . . leadership is at its best when it is rooted in* **COMPASSION** *and humility."* **LETTER 13 (M. J. SMITH):** *"It summons us to create policies and practices that are commensurate with sightedness and non-victim-blaming* **COMPASSION**.*"* **LETTER 28 (CHILCOTE):** *"This reign of shalom for which we all yearn points to the gift of reconciliation, the practices of justice and* **COMPASSION,** *and the flowering of peace and joy."* **LETTER 51 (SHERMA):** *"In a time of climate change and environmental degradation, a spirituality of place could move us towards care and* **COMPASSION** *naturally."* **LETTER 59 (RIZWAN):** *"May God Almighty bless you and guide you in your actions towards a more just and* **COMPASSIONATE** *society."* **LETTER 67 (GYATSO):** *". . . Shantideva urges us to cultivate* **COMPASSION** *as much as we can."* **LETTER 80 (EASTON-FLAKE):** *". . . we must extend* **COMPASSION** *across national borders."* ★

RELIGIOUS VOICES: DAYS 51–60

LETTER 51 | MARCH 11, 2021

Rita D. Sherma

Director and Associate Professor of Hindu Studies, Mira and Ajay Shingal Center for Dharma Studies, Graduate Theological Union

LETTER 52 | MARCH 12, 2021

Aaron Koller

Professor of Near Eastern Studies, Yeshiva University

LETTER 53 | MARCH 13, 2021

Nirinjan Kaur Khalsa-Baker

Senior Instructor Theological Studies, Loyola Marymount University

LETTER 54 | MARCH 14, 2021

William P. Brown

William Marcellus McPheeters Professor of Old Testament, Columbia Theological Seminary

LETTER 55 | MARCH 15, 2021

Herbert Robinson Marbury

Associate Professor of Hebrew Bible and Ancient Near East, Vanderbilt University Divinity School

LETTER 56 | MARCH 16, 2021

Julie Faith Parker

Associate Professor of Biblical Studies, The General Theological Seminary of the Episcopal Church

LETTER 57 | MARCH 17, 2021

Eric Daryl Meyer

Gregory Roeben and Susan Raunig Professor of Social Justice and the Human-Animal Relationship, Carroll College

LETTER 58 | MARCH 18, 2021

Christine Hayes

Sterling Professor of Religious Studies in Classical Judaica, Yale University

LETTER 59 | MARCH 19, 2021

Syed Atif Rizwan

Assistant Professor of Islamic and Interreligious Studies; Director of the Catholic-Muslim Studies Program, Catholic Theological Union

LETTER 60 | MARCH 20, 2021

Rebecca Epstein-Levi

Mellon Assistant Professor of Jewish Studies and Gender and Sexuality Studies, Vanderbilt University

Dear President Biden, Vice President Harris, and Members of the 117th Congress,

It is often said that diversity is America's strength. But it cannot be a strength if it is penalized and pulverized; this is the danger of *triumphalism*. It also cannot be our strength if diversity is maintained in siloed solitudes; this is the danger of cultural *disjunction*.

Diversity can only strengthen the fabric of America if its many-hued dreams are interlaced in the warp and weft of America's tapestry. Then, a complex cultural strength results—vivid with many imaginings and yearnings. As President Lyndon B. Johnson reminded us in his January 20, 1965, inaugural address: "They came here—the exile and the stranger, brave but frightened—to find a place where a man could be his own man. They made a covenant with this land. Conceived in justice, written in liberty, bound in union, it was meant one day to inspire the hopes of all mankind; and it binds us still. If we keep its terms, we shall flourish."

But how are we to move beyond individual dreams to shared visions? In this quest, a theology of the land beckons. In a time of climate change and environmental degradation, a spirituality of place could move us towards care and compassion naturally, as we sense a "belonging" to the beauty that is America's geography.

As a Hindu American theologian, I traverse by the light of the principle that holds as sacred the intrinsic value of the plenitude of divine creativity on Earth. The purpose that gives meaning to life is, thus, the quest for communion with the Divine—experienced through intimacy with creation. The fabric of this ancient faith contains key strands interwoven with gratitude for, and profound interrelationship with, the natural world. This telos, to find transcendence in immanence, is well reflected in an ancient hymn from the canonical Sanskrit text, Yajur Veda (36:17), which evinces an intertwined existence with the living world:

> May peace sweep through the skies and universally across the immense spaces
> May there be peace on earth, peace in the waters, peace in all herbal plants,
> peace and flourishing in the trees and forests
> May the divine realms be inundated with tranquility
> In all that exists, everywhere, may there be peace
> May all be calm and ever-serene
> *Om*, peace in all levels of existence!
> *(Translation by R. D. Sherma)*

DAY 52, LETTER 52

Aaron Koller

Dear President Biden, Vice President Harris, and Members of the 117th Congress,

You have the imperative and daunting task of healing a nation wounded by a pandemic, by tribalism, by a new world order leaving so many of us behind. Our great country is founded on ideals that have been a beacon to the world and a guiding light for our own nation. How can we heal and make sure that light continues to shine brightly?

A rabbinic text about how to respond when encountering a beggar on the street—for many of us, an all-too-common occurrence—offers an answer. Leviticus Rabbah 34:7 teaches that the first thing to do is to listen carefully to what the poor person says. The Midrash imagines such an individual crying out: "Look at me! Look at what I was, and look at what I am now."

> **But the act of looking … is central to the practice of charity.**

It is so natural to avert one's eyes from someone on the subway or sidewalk asking for money. But the act of looking—simply observing that this is a person before me—is central to the practice of charity. Looking at the face of a person in need means grappling with that individual's personhood. This decenters our sense of the world, which can be disconcerting.

But this looking—this seeing the eyes, this recognition of the humanity of the person in front of us—is also the beginning of all empathy, the beginning of all ethics, the beginning of all understanding.

So this is what we, the nation, ask of you, our leaders: *Look at us*. See us for who we are, for who we were, and for who we can be. See us as individuals, as a collective, as similar and different. Do not see us as voters, but as people. And think of those millions of faces, those 700 million individual eyes upon you, as you make decisions that will affect us all. Look at us, as we look to you.

Nirinjan Kaur Khalsa-Baker

Dear President Biden, Vice President Harris, and Members of the 117th Congress,

Sat Siri Akal, as a Sikh I greet you by acknowledging that "Truth is Timeless."

You have been handed a heavy burden to care for our country and its people at a time when so many are divided by social inequalities, economic inequities, and contesting claims to the truth. We see fear and violence erupt from broken systems that, for too long, have not served "We the People."

How can we find common ground in the American dream of life, liberty, and the pursuit of happiness? How can we reconcile centuries of abuse with the vision of democracy and equality that we hold to be true and self-evident? How can we traverse the ocean of disinformation and build bridges over dark chasms of distrust?

We turn to the light of religious wisdoms to guide us through this darkness …

We turn to the light of religious wisdoms to guide us through this darkness as we rebirth our country. This transformation requires a change of heart, mind, and action to heal old wounds, serve one another, and protect the dignity of all life.

Sikh wisdom teaches us to be humble students, selfless servants, sovereign sages, and fearless warriors. By cultivating a meditative mind, we develop discernment to see beyond human constructed divisions. Guru Nanak, the first Sikh Guru, proclaims: "The highest yoga practice is to see the kinship of humankind; by conquering your mind, you conquer the world" (*Guru Granth*, 6).

By looking beyond our self-centered ego, we see the interconnectedness of all life (*Ik Ong Kar*). By letting go of fear (*nirbhao*), we no longer see others as enemies (*nirvair*), and we come together in beloved community (*sangat*). Guru Arjan teaches: "I have forgotten my envy of others since I have realized the divine company. I see no enemy. I see no stranger. We all belong to one another" (*Guru Granth*, 1299).

Sikhi offers a way of being in the world that is both sovereign and interconnected, exemplified as the Warrior Sage who shows up with a courageous heart and a discerning mind, to care for and defend the dignity of all life. May your tenure be guided by this spirit to bring peace and prosperity to all.

Nanak Nam — In the vibration of the One
Chardi Kala — Ever rising spirit
Tere Bhane — By your grace
Sarbat Da Bhala — May all prosper in peace

DAY 54, LETTER 54

William P. Brown

Dear President Biden, Vice President Harris, and Members of the 117th Congress,

You have inherited a demoralized and fractured nation. It is hard to see a way forward when so many citizens distrust each other, even resorting to violence. May the God of all nations bless you with wisdom, courage, and the desire for justice.

This past year reminds me of the Israelites wandering in the wilderness, a place of testing, division, and conflict (Exodus 16–19; Numbers 10–36). The wilderness period was a time of countless failures and missteps, intransigence and denial. Worst of all was the Israelites' stubbornness in their desire to return to Egypt, the place of their enslavement, when faced with the physical challenges and difficult truths of the wilderness (Exodus 17:3; Numbers 11:5, 18–20; 14:2–4; 20:5).

America's pandemic "wilderness" offers its own set of painful truths. The "knee" of white supremacy continues to crush the lives of Black men and women. Under the thumb of human supremacy, the climate responds with devastating consequences. Ignorant, hate-filled rhetoric can lead to violence to the point of dismantling our democracy. The coronavirus has exposed the multiple pandemics of racism, poverty, polarizing division, and environmental degradation. The pressing question today is: do we try to go back to "business as usual" of pre-pandemic days, or do we move forward toward a more just, equitable, and environmentally sound future?

> **America's pandemic "wilderness" offers its own set of painful truths.**

At the end of their forty-year plight in wilderness, Moses implored the Israelites: "Remember that you were a slave in the land of Egypt" (Deuteronomy 5:15). "Remember the long way that the Lord your God has led you these forty years in the wilderness" (Deuteronomy 8:2). Such remembrance was meant to ensure that out of experience and empathy, we would protect the most vulnerable (Exodus 22:21–23; 23:9).

May we remember. The year 2020 confirmed how vulnerable all of us are, but some more than others, from essential workers to communities of color. Let us not forget as we move toward America's promise that "the pursuit of happiness" is to be shared by all in a land that flourishes, the wilderness included.

Herbert Robinson Marbury

Dear President Biden, Vice President Harris, and Members of the 117th Congress,

On the journey from bondage to freedom, the Israelites camp at Paran, where they look across the horizon and survey Canaan for the first time. The land flows with the possibilities of "milk and honey" (Numbers 13:27). A new life awaits them—if they have the vision and wherewithal to grasp it. Sadly, they do not. The Israelites see what appear to be giants in the land—obstacles so large that they feel small and ineffectual in comparison. They respond with sad resignation: "We seemed as grasshoppers to ourselves and so we seemed to them" (Numbers 13:33). Because their vision is too small to meet the challenge of their day, they end up wandering for the next forty years, a lost generation of possibility.

> **"**
>
> *Our challenges today also appear to be giants…*

Our challenges today also appear to be giants. Our public education system has been gutted by the previous administration. Its policies sacrificed both the well-being of our teachers—some of our most intrepid public servants—and the life chances of our poorest children. The repressive violence of our policing structures has proliferated so that it can no longer be corrected simply by retraining individual "good" officers. White nationalism has become our dominant terrorist threat. Health care, a basic right of every child of God, remains the property of the privileged. A full day's work does not afford countless people a living wage, and the margin of wage disparity for women—especially women of color—is simply unconscionable. And finally, God's earth, of which we are all stewards, groans on the brink of irreparable damage.

These are the mighty giants *we* face. They dominate the landscape of our nation's political, economic, and social horizons. Enact policies that are large enough to meet the challenges that our giants present. Recall examples such as FDR's New Deal, LBJ's Medicare, and Barack Obama's Affordable Care Act. Perhaps this means that your vision must be larger than you expected.

We stand at the precipice of decision: we can see a land of new possibilities, or we can cower and lose a generation to wandering. The choice is yours. Look across the horizon to the land that lies beyond the River Jordan and boldly lead this nation to face our giants.

Julie Faith Parker

Dear President Biden, Vice President Harris, and Members of the 117th Congress,

Thank you.

Along with countless people not only in this nation, but around the globe, I am grateful for your courage, dedication, sacrifice, intellect, experience, creativity, and innovation. The American people look to you to lead and guide us in fostering acts of kindness and legislating offerings of hope for a deeply weary world.

Stories invite us to experience empathy; perhaps this is why Scripture is full of them. So I would like to share with you a little-known story from the Hebrew Bible. In 2 Kings 5:1–14, we meet an anonymous young Israelite girl who has been taken captive by raiders and brought north to Aram. In this foreign land, she becomes a servant for the wife of a military commander named Naaman, who suffers from leprosy. The Israelite slave girl expresses a wish that Naaman might be healed by the Israelite prophet Elisha: "O that my lord were with the prophet who is in Samaria, then he would cure him of his leprosy!" Naaman speaks to his king and then journeys to Samaria to see Elisha, who conveys that Naaman must immerse himself in the Jordan River seven times. At first Naaman resists; but once he follows through on the prophetic instructions, he is cured.

> *... remember the most vulnerable among us whom we so easily forget.*

In this way, the episode ends happily, as hopes for healing—which we understand only too well—are fulfilled. But the characters in the story, along with innumerable Bible readers and commentators, often forget about the brave, resilient, caring Israelite slave girl who speaks up and suggests a way to cure Naaman's illness.

I implore you to please remember the most vulnerable among us whom we so easily forget. They too have a lot to offer. Listen to their stories and value their advice. Share their testimonies in ways that will lead us to act with compassion for others.

For reasons well known, the task before you is daunting. Yet, along with my siblings in this nation, I will join with you and do my part. Together may we create a nation that is generous with kindness.

Eric Daryl Meyer

Dear President Biden, Vice President Harris, and Members of the 117th Congress,

I write to you from the Christian tradition, from a Catholic college in Montana, on land that historically supported Salish and Blackfeet people, whose struggle and memory I strive to honor.

Scripture often depicts divine justice as a stunning reversal of fortunes. It is a source of comfort, but not to everyone. Hannah has seen God's work and concludes: "Those who were full have hired themselves out for bread, but those who were hungry are fat with spoil" (1 Samuel 2:5). Similarly, Jesus tells his followers: "Many who are first will be last, and many who are last will be first" (Matthew 19:30). Jesus' Sermon on the Plain also upends social status: "Blessed are you who are poor … but woe to you who are rich" (Luke 6:20, 24). These are hard teachings.

> **To protect the land is to care for the poor.**

Human justice ought to echo and emulate divine justice, even in such reversals—a responsibility that the Catholic tradition names as "the preferential option for the poor." This means that wherever we have choices, we should prioritize those with the least access to society's goods. This work entails redistributing social resources to empower the disenfranchised. Further, it entails cultivating a perspectival solidarity that sees tax codes, environmental regulations, and housing policies through the eyes of those they affect most intimately.

At present, the preferential option points us toward those burdened by bias and discrimination, those abandoned by social safety nets, and those left behind by economic recovery. Accordingly, I would urge you to welcome immigrants, raise the minimum wage, combat wealth inequality, refuse to tolerate racial inequities, and strengthen legal protections for the LGBTQ community.

Moreover, as Pope Francis insists in the encyclical letter *Laudato Si'*, the earth itself and nonhuman creatures are among the poor to whom we owe a special responsibility. This is not a separate matter. Clean air, fresh water, healthy food, and good soil are especially pressing concerns to our poorest human neighbors who cannot insulate themselves from ecological catastrophe with wealth. We all belong to the earth, dust from which we rise and into which we fall. To protect the land is to care for the poor.

Remembering that God's justice attends to the poor, I urge you to hold yourself accountable to such justice.

DAY 58, LETTER 58

Christine Hayes

Dear President Biden, Vice President Harris, and Members of the 117th Congress,

Justice and mercy are complementary moral virtues. Their complementary nature finds expression in the biblical characterization of God as a god of justice and mercy (Deuteronomy 4:31; 32:4; Isaiah 30:18; Psalm 89:14 [Hebrew 89:15]) and in the writings of the Hebrew prophets, who summoned both righteousness and loving-kindness as they fought for the soul of their nation (Micah 6:8; Zechariah 7:9).

President Biden, you have promised to fight for the soul of this nation. As our country struggles to recover its purpose and promise, this will require the twinned virtues of justice and mercy.

Justice, grounded in *truth*, makes social relationships possible through a commitment to what is fair and right. A cynical disregard for truth, magnified by technologies of unprecedented power and reach, has undermined trust in the nation's imperfect but ever aspiring institutions, fueling the rise of domestic terrorism from anti-government and white supremacist groups. Restoring trust in our institutions, a commitment to our common humanity, and civility in the public square means holding the purveyors of falsehood accountable for their words and actions. Those who promote the "Big Lie" of election fraud and other falsifiable claims and grievances must be held accountable for the terror and violence their words have unleashed. We have seen these lies crumble at the bar of justice, because justice demands truth.

> *Justice and mercy are complementary moral virtues.*

But fighting for the soul of the nation will also require mercy. Mercy, grounded in *love*, restores ruptured relationships through a commitment to compassion and forgiveness. Jewish tradition teaches that forgiveness is a duty. Once an offender has borne the consequences of their wrongdoing, redressed injuries, and sought forgiveness, it is forbidden for the injured to be hard-hearted (Mishnah Bava Qamma 8:7).

Our nation *requires* justice and *needs* mercy. An ancient Jewish tradition compares God at the moment of creation to a king holding a delicate glass (Genesis Rabbah 12:15). The glass will shatter if filled with hot liquid or cold liquid, so the king mixes hot and cold. Similarly, God realized that if God created the world with mercy only, wickedness would abound; with justice only, it would not long endure. And so, God created the world with both justice and mercy, in the fervent hope that the world might endure.

DAY 59, LETTER 59

Syed Atif Rizwan

Dear President Biden, Vice President Harris, and Members of the 117th Congress,

May God's infinite peace, compassion, and blessings be upon all of you.

It would be unremarkable to state that we are living in a moment that demands more precise attention to the plight of Americans, especially those belonging to communities of color. Each citizen is deserving of and can rightfully demand institutions and policies grounded in justice.

The most recurring concept in the Holy Qur'an is the belief in the oneness of God. The second most recurring concept is justice. Importantly, both belief and justice appear together in verse after verse. For example, chapter 4, verse 135, states: "You who believe, uphold justice and bear witness to God, even if it is against yourselves, your parents, or your relatives. Whether the person is rich or poor, God can take care of them best. Do not let your own desires swerve you away from justice. If you distort or neglect justice, God is fully aware of what you do." And chapter 5, verse 8, states: "You who believe … do not let hatred of others lead you away from justice. Adhere to justice, for it is closer to piety."

> **Each citizen is deserving of … institutions and policies grounded in justice.**

The message from these verses is clear: To be a believer is to be just. And to be just is to be a believer. As you steward our nation, I hope that you will use your privilege to do what is necessary to lift up those who are less fortunate than some of us because of the systemic ways in which they have been denied justice. As the Prophet Muḥammad (may God's peace and blessings be upon him) says in a teaching that reflects the Golden Rule: "No one is a true believer until they want for their sisters and brothers what they want for themselves" *(Ṣaḥīḥ al-Bukhārī)*.

May God Almighty bless you and guide you in your actions towards a more just and compassionate society.

Rebecca Epstein-Levi

Dear President Biden, Vice President Harris, and Members of the 117th Congress,

I voted for you because I knew countless lives depended on it.

Two months into your administration, I am angry.

As an ethicist, I want to tell you several things. I want to tell you to give *everyone* substantial and ongoing COVID relief *without* means-testing, to do more, faster, to expand high-quality health care to more people, and to prioritize vaccine distribution for the Black, Brown, Indigenous, undocumented, and disabled people who have suffered disproportionately during this pandemic.

I want to tell you not to back down on raising the federal minimum wage or on student debt relief, to fight harder to end deportations, to act decisively to close detention facilities. I want to tell you to withhold the power and resources of the state from policing and incarceration, and to use those to give everyone the resources they need to thrive.

> *... reject the temptation to make idols of unity, compromise, and, above all, the political status quo.*

Yet, though I write here as a *Jewish* ethicist, I cannot name any specific text or ritual that unambiguously instructs the federal government, for example, to simply give people money, although I believe, as a Jew and as a Jewish ethicist, that the federal government is morally obligated to do just that.

I can, however, say my tradition abhors idolatry above nearly all else. Indeed, Babylonian Talmud Yoma 82a tells us that the prohibition against idol worship is one of only three commandments that one may not break to save a life. Why? If we understand idolatry as valuing anything above the image of God, and if we understand human lives as being in the image of God (Genesis 1:27), then to place anything, however lofty or well-intentioned, ahead of those lives is to commit idolatry.

So what I have said amounts to this: You must reject the temptation to make idols of unity, compromise, and, above all, the political status quo. There must be no unity or compromise with white supremacists, fascists, or their legislative allies and enablers. Nor must you place "normalcy" ahead of giving people what they need to survive, let alone flourish.

You must, rather, remember that the image of God lies *not* in "unity" or "civility" or "normalcy," but in the countless lives that depend on you.

Letter 42 / Lewis

"Jesus knew well the human tendency to circumvent the capacity of God's *love*."

Letter 21 / Hogan

"But what does *love* of one's neighbor actually look like, in the realm of politics?"

Letter 20 / Barreto

"Embody a politics in which belonging, justice, and *love* crowd out fear, self-interest, and the vain pursuit of power."

Letter 22 / Eskenazi & Wright

"At its center are laws and statutes demanding *love* for neighbor and stranger."

Letter 75 / Good

"As Song of Songs reminds us: '*love* is strong as death' (8:6)."

Letter 62 / Kemp

"May we all work in hope, pray in faith, and speak truth in *love*."

RELIGIOUS VOICES: DAYS 61–70

LETTER 61 | MARCH 21, 2021

Naomi Koltun-Fromm

Associate Professor of Religion, Haverford College

LETTER 62 | MARCH 22, 2021

Joel B. Kemp

Assistant Professor of Hebrew Bible, Emory University's Candler School of Theology

LETTER 63 | MARCH 23, 2021

Phillis Isabella Sheppard

E. Rhodes and Leona B. Carpenter Associate Professor of Religion, Psychology, and Culture, Vanderbilt University Divinity School

LETTER 64 | MARCH 24, 2021

Eric Haruki Swanson

Assistant Professor of Theological Studies, Loyola Marymount University

LETTER 65 | MARCH 25, 2021

Grace Song

Won Buddhist Studies Department Chair, Won Institute of Graduate Studies

LETTER 66 | MARCH 26, 2021

Tammy Jacobowitz

Bible Department Chair, SAR High School

LETTER 67 | MARCH 27, 2021

Janet Gyatso

Hershey Professor of Buddhist Studies and Associate Dean for Faculty and Academic Affairs, Harvard Divinity School

LETTER 68 | MARCH 28, 2021

Cecilia González-Andrieu

Professor of Theology, Loyola Marymount University

LETTER 69 | MARCH 29, 2021

Kenneth Ngwa

Associate Professor of Hebrew Bible, Drew University Theological School

LETTER 70 | MARCH 30, 2021

Angela N. Parker

Assistant Professor of New Testament and Greek, Mercer University's McAfee School of Theology

Naomi Koltun-Fromm

Dear President Biden, Vice President Harris, and Members of the 117th Congress,

Our electoral campaigning process tends to favor candidates who come out strongly as being pro-this or anti-that. Taking a strong stand often wins an election.

Yet governing a democracy is messy. Often, leaders must compromise in order to move forward; but many elected leaders resist forgoing their ideals, even if or when those ideals—as lofty as they may be—stand in the way of actually governing. We have witnessed how deleterious such grandstanding and obstructionism can be to the functioning of governance and the administration of the basic needs of all Americans, from health care and social security, to education, housing and more.

> *…a narrow-minded principled stand … can have serious consequences.*

The ancient rabbis narrate a story that illustrates the ultimate futility of overplaying one's principles and ideals. Babylonian Talmud Gittin 55b describes how the Second Temple was destroyed by the Romans as the result of several interconnected self-aggrandizing and over-principled stands taken by the people of Jerusalem and their leaders, the Temple authorities. In this text, the rabbis relate a complicated story in which a series of misguided events leads the Romans to test the Jerusalemites' loyalty by sending a sacrifice to the Temple. Because Bar Kamtza, the man who prompts the Romans to send the sacrifice, previously had been humiliated by a fellow Jerusalemite without local leaders interceding on his behalf, he purposefully damages the animal, knowing it will be rejected. When the Temple authorities discover Bar Kamtza's duplicity, they stand on their ritual-legal principles and reject the sacrifice, which causes the Romans to destroy the Temple in the ensuing war.

The religious authorities in this story show a lack of moral leadership, with devastating consequences. We tend to admire those who lead by their principles, and even personal faith; but in our vast, diverse, and beautifully multicultural country, a narrow-minded principled stand, no matter how noble, can have serious consequences. Moral leadership in America sometimes means stepping outside of one's personal faith, ideology, or worldview in order to protect and uplift the whole community.

DAY 62, LETTER 62

Joel B. Kemp

Dear President Biden, Vice President Harris, and Members of the 117th Congress,

As you assume the daunting task of serving a nation reeling from tragedies and smoldering with discontent, let me assure you that the prayers of many people of faith accompany you on this journey. As I reflect on this moment in American history, we find ourselves confronting fundamental questions about who we are and what we want to be. The persistence of racial injustices, economic inequalities, political polarization, and the deaths of over 500,000 Americans because of COVID-19 have produced a palpable sense of despair and anxiety in this nation. How should you meet this moment? How might you provide hope and comfort for a nation in desperate need of both?

> " ... we must never allow despair, violence, and hatred to have the final word.

As a Christian minister and scholar of the Hebrew Bible (Old Testament), I often turn to Scripture to find answers. Like our country today, the prophet Ezekiel addressed a nation wrestling with loss and struggling to find hope amidst great suffering. Ezekiel captures the nation's despair and desperation when he quotes how the people are feeling: "Our bones are dried up, and our hope is lost; we are cut off completely" (37:11). In this oft-cited passage, Ezekiel sees a valley of dry bones and hears God ask: "Can these bones live?" (37:3). What follows is a fantastic vision of restoration and quasi-resurrection. A nation greatly divided and left for dead is reanimated and united.

While Ezekiel 37 emphasizes God's miraculous intervention, it also reminds us that humans have a role to play in this restoration. Like the prophet, we must be willing to see and be present among those who are suffering. We must choose to speak while others are silent. We must choose to see what is possible when others only see the problems. Above all, we must never allow despair, violence, and hatred to have the final word.

In closing, I join other contributors in encouraging you to work courageously, creatively, and compassionately to inspire "the better angels of our nature." May we all work in hope, pray in faith, and speak truth in love.

Dear President Biden, Vice President Harris, and Members of the 117th Congress,

On January 6, 2021, our nation witnessed the violent attempt to not only overturn the presidential election but to rewrite history. The insurrectionists claimed the election had been stolen; so, as perceived victims, they believed they had a right to turn Capitol Hill into the battleground for *their* vision of this country.

Proverbs 29:18 warns: "Without a vision, the people perish" (King James Version). Another translation reads: "Without a vision the people lose restraint" (U.S. Conference of Catholic Bishops). A third version declares: "Where there is no prophecy, the people cast off restraint" (New Revised Standard Version). All three translations are apropos to our current moment.

> *You must eradicate the mechanisms of injustice …*

This biblical verse and the events of January 6 warn us of what can happen when leadership lacks a vision—not just any vision, but a prophetic vision.

Today we need prophetic leadership that can repent for past wrongs and articulate a vision of a more inclusive and just United States. We need leaders who open their eyes to the injustices across our country. We need leaders who see that families are still trying to find their stolen children at the borders of this country. We need leaders who see that women are still victims of harassment and subjected to violence every nine seconds, especially transgender women of color. We need leaders who see that Black and Brown bodies are used for target practice by those who carry badges and guns and that Black and Brown people are living in a medical apartheid. We need leaders who see that our most "essential workers" earn less than a living wage and many others cannot even find a job.

The work ahead of you will be arduous. The change in administrations has not silenced or impeded the organizing of those who let loose restraint and nearly overturned our democratic processes on January 6. You must eradicate the mechanisms of injustice that are, quite frankly, in the DNA of this country and that permeate government, education, and religious deliberations and processes.

We are a country at war with itself. We need your prophetic leadership and vision of justice, inclusivity, truth, and hope for the future of the United States.

Dear President Biden, Vice President Harris, and Members of the 117th Congress,

On Inauguration Day, President Biden recognized our current historical moment as one of "crisis and challenge," calling upon the nation to see that "unity is the path forward." While the message brought about a feeling of optimism for the future of this nation, it saddens me to see the persistence of the divisive rhetoric that continues to plague our public and private discourse, drowning out all calls for unity.

As a multiracial Asian American, I feel the physical violence and vile words directed at our fellow citizens to "Go back to your country" reverberate within me, conjuring up the moments in my life that challenged my understanding of what it means to be an American. As a nation, we uphold justice and equality as our core values, and yet we continue to witness moments in which we must question whether these ideals ring true for all of us.

> *... the profound truth of our shared humanity is always present ...*

How can we open our hearts and respond to the calls for unity when they continue to be muffled by the voices of hatred, greed, and ignorance? The Buddhist tradition has long recognized the necessity to combat these poisons. The first fascicle of the *Mahāvairocana-sūtra* begins with an exposition on the nature of our mind, suggesting that the profound truth of our shared humanity is always present, not only in the mind of the Buddhist practitioner, but also in the minds of all sentient beings regardless of who they are or where they stand. The task given to the practitioner is not only for one to realize this truth within themselves, but also to have the courage, perseverance, and compassion to help others. This arduous path must begin with the recognition of the fundamental humanity we all share.

As we all work to heal our nation, I humbly ask that we each carefully examine our own actions and words as we help one another recognize our interdependent and shared humanity, not only as a goal to achieve in the future, but as the foundation on which we stand as we move forward.

Dear President Biden, Vice President Harris, and Members of the 117th Congress,

The Vietnamese poet Ocean Vuong shares a story of his mother attending his poetry reading and not understanding a word but sobbing at the end. "What did I do?" he asked. She replied: "No, I just never thought I'd live to see all these white people clapping for my son." He sat with her words for a while, trying to understand the meaning of this kind of validation. The next day at his mother's nail salon, he watched her kneel at the pedicure chair before one white woman after another. She was below their eye level for so many years. He finally understood what it meant for her to be in a space where people saw her, face-to-face, as an equal.

Asian immigrants like the Vuongs come to the United States with hopes for a brighter future. But they enter a country with structural racial inequities that make Asians invisible and the racism against them hidden. Enough is enough. As a country, we must pay attention to the violence against Asian Americans and amplify the injustices that have been going on for far too long.

I turn to the Won Buddhist founding motive, which directs us to "lead all sentient beings, who are drowning in the turbulent sea of suffering, to a vast and immeasurable paradise." The "paradise" Won Buddhists speak of is one founded on treating all people with dignity and respect and building a fair and equitable society. Our interdependent existence requires us to cut through our individual and social ego and wake up to the reality that there is no neutral. Oppression of one group entails oppression for all. If we do not work towards collective liberation, then we are failing as political and religious leaders.

Let us remember that one thought leads to who we become, so may we move forward with compassion and embodied wisdom. In the words of the Buddha from *The Dhammapada*:

> The thought manifests the word;
> The word manifests the deed;
> The deed develops into habit;
> And habit hardens into character;
> So watch the thought and its ways with care,
> And let them spring forth from love
> Born out of compassion for all beings.
> As the shadow follows the body, as we think, so we become.

Dear President Biden, Vice President Harris, and Members of the 117th Congress,

Throughout the Hebrew Bible, prophets warn of the dangers of an inflated ego, which misleads leaders to think they can be fully self-reliant. The illusion of self-sufficiency means a leader won't benefit from the abundant resources that others provide, which can lead to myopia, poor judgment, and much worse.

By contrast, humility—living with awareness of one's strengths and limitations—is the birthplace of stable, capable leadership. With humility comes slowness and deliberation. To be humble is to understand that no one person, team, or group holds a monopoly on answers or insight.

But can one have too much humility?

The Pentateuch praises the towering leader, Moses, for his humility: "Now Moses was a very humble man, more so than any other person on earth" (Numbers 12:3). Though his list of accomplishments staggers the human imagination, not the least of which was meeting God "face to face" (Exodus 33:11), Moses did not broadcast his successes. On the contrary, all who met him encountered a man with inner reserve.

> **Leadership cannot be an exercise of the ego ...**

But the rabbis of the Midrash, an ancient collection of biblical interpretation, expose the fault lines of Moses' humility. On the opening verse of Leviticus, the rabbis highlight God's call to Moses: "The Lord called to Moses and spoke to him from the Tent of Meeting" (Leviticus 1:1). They inflect the call as an impatient nudge, as if to say: "Moses! Enough humility! For too long, you have stood at the sidelines rather than step up to the plate. At the sea, I coaxed you to raise your staff. At Mount Sinai, you ascended only by invitation. I call you now because it is you and only you who can hear My voice. Step up, please. Come closer." The lesson from the rabbis in Leviticus Rabbah 1:5 is that excessive humility can slide into self-doubt and failure to act.

In this challenging moment, balance self-reliance with the recognition that you do not have all the answers. Honor your wisdom and lean into your resources. Leadership cannot be an exercise of the ego, but must involve stepping up to meet an urgent demand. If you wait, the moment will pass you by.

DAY 67, LETTER 67

Janet Gyatso

Dear President Biden, Vice President Harris, and Members of the 117th Congress,

It gives great hope to us all to have leaders such as yourselves. We are grateful to know you are dedicated and serious about trying to solve the problems of our time. For it can no longer be denied that our world—our very planet—now faces unprecedented challenges, challenges to the very survival of humanity and the ongoing viability of the earth. The sentient creatures of our planet, human beings and other animals alike, face enormous suffering if we do not address those issues. In fact, people and other animals are already experiencing untold agonies as a result of the greed, animosity, and ignorance of some human beings, all of which are only getting greater in the 21st century.

> *The key is to be able to see from the point of view of others …*

The classic Buddhist treatise on compassion for others, *Bodhicharya Avatara*, written by Shantideva in India in the eighth century CE, acknowledges how hard it is for anyone to truly care for another as much as they care for themselves. He marvels even at the very possibility of having leaders who can actually hear the pain of others. As he writes: "Such a being, unprecedented, an excellent jewel, in whom there is born concern for others such as others have not even for themselves, how is such a being born?" (1.25). The work goes on to teach its readers how to cultivate the capacity to sustain genuine altruistic care.

While that goal is hard to actualize perfectly, Shantideva urges us to cultivate compassion as much as we can. The key is to be able to see from the point of view of others, and to place our own narrow perspectives into question. That includes—especially for a society, or a country, or a corporation—seeing the harm we cause in service of our own selfish gain. Shantideva asks himself, and his fellow humans, on behalf of the less fortunate beings of the world: "Where can fish and other creatures be taken where I might not kill them?" (5.11). In an era of diminishing resources, we are fortunate to have leaders like you who are willing to take on an ethical perspective that benefits all of our fellow sentient beings.

Cecilia González-Andrieu

Dear President Biden, Vice President Harris, and Members of the 117th Congress,

I am an educator who works with young people. Living in Los Angeles brings the invitation to not just coexist, but to thrive together in the midst of our extraordinary diversity. Honoring this in our classrooms, we engage in a practice we call "CIQs" as a way to engage reality and remain awake to it, while resisting the numbness of feeling overwhelmed.

We begin with "C": challenges, experiences that turn our world upside down and present a new vantage point we had not considered. We see this in Jesus' many parables, as he upends expectations, blowing his hearers' minds in the process (Luke 15:3–10). You mean the father should really welcome his wayward son, and do so without judgment (Luke 15:11–32)? Jesus' challenge was to see the world as God does, pushing us past *what is*, to dream of what *could be*. May you be constantly challenged by the perspectives of those who, lacking power, see reality more clearly.

> **The roaring fire of an insight is built from the sparks lighting up in each of us.**

We follow with the "I": insights. The roaring fire of an insight is built from the sparks lighting up in each of us. Insights grow from the past, take a sobering look at the present, and then orient us to a longed-for future. Insights are built in community, in dialogue, in conversation. Jesus ignites such insights by judging the moment through appealing to his community's wisdom. When he walks with despondent travelers who believe he is dead, he invites them to engage their intellect along with their hearts through conversation, a journey, a meal (Luke 24:13–35). May you experience incandescent insights, with your eyes fixed on the common good and ready to contribute a spark of hope to the world.

We end with "Q": questions. Young people often feel silenced and irrelevant, but encouraging questions lets them know they are welcomed, needed, celebrated, because their questions are the ground from which new challenges are articulated, and working together may grow into insights. In his daily practice, Jesus embraced questions—of himself, God, others (for example, Luke 10:25–37). As he dreamed of a different world, he encouraged questions as a sure sign of faith. May you ask very productive questions as you serve our country in our extraordinary diversity.

DAY 69, LETTER 69

Kenneth Ngwa

Dear President Biden, Vice President Harris, and Members of the 117th Congress,

As you continue with the enormous task of governing to "Build Back Better," I encourage you to constantly remember those whom President Biden repeatedly described during his campaign as the "backbone" of the nation: the middle class. And I urge you to extend that focus to the poor and all those whose lives have been crushed by longstanding adverse policies and prejudices, which you are in a position to redesign.

The writers of the biblical Exodus story tell of a people that had fallen under the spell of xenophobic sentiments, economic hardship, ethno-nationalist political ideology, a massive health pandemic, and ecological devastation. Pharaoh mobilized his people, put specific laws in place, and created an enslaving structure for the Israelites. These realities made life "bitter" for the Hebrews (Exodus 1:14) and required a major redesign of the governing philosophy and praxis.

> *...be brave and take actions that sustain life...*

The first task of that redesign fell on the midwives, Shiphrah and Puah. Because they stayed connected to the suffering masses, heard their voices, and felt their pain, they stood up to Pharaoh: "The midwives, fearing God, did not do as the king of Egypt had told them; they let the boys live" (Exodus 1:17). God then took notice of the people's suffering (Exodus 2:25); and at the burning bush, God revealed a plan to Moses to liberate the people (Exodus 3), a plan recounted in the Passover ritual.

I encourage you to follow the tradition of the midwives: be brave and take actions that sustain life. Move your agenda beyond repairing our nation, to redesigning it toward justice and equity. Commit to the equally urgent and ardent work of sustained investment in the lives, communities, and ingenuity of those who have been crushed by the longstanding racism, sexism, xenophobia, ethno-nationalism, health disparities, and ecological devastation.

May you institutionalize the ways historically marginalized people are actually and really the builders of its democracy. May you show us how, together, we can reject racism, embody generosity, and create a better life for all.

Dear President Biden, Vice President Harris, and Members of the 117th Congress,

Growing up, I remember singing hymns with lines like, "You can't beat God's giving, no matter how you try" or asking myself, is my "all on the altar of sacrifice"? As a divorced mother of two, I often sang these lyrics while driving my minivan with the gas gauge hovering on "E" for empty. In the United States of America, Black women tend to be breadwinning mothers more so than other racially identified women. Prior to obtaining my PhD in New Testament, I remember those days well.

In Mark 12:41–44, Jesus praises a widow who placed two small coins into the treasury. Noting that the rich gave "out of their abundance," Jesus says that she gave "her whole existence." Commentators commend the woman because she gave at such great personal cost. I have a difficult time with that reading. Prior to the widow's offering, in Mark 12:38–40, Jesus denounces scribes who "devour widows' houses," meaning that the scribes often took material advantage of widows by overtaxing them to the point of unpayable debts and subsequent destitution.

> *… focus our collective attention on the women who are being left behind.*

One lesson here is that people have value, aside from their financial circumstances. Another takeaway is that the most vulnerable in society require protections, particularly the right to earn substantial living wages.

According to one study, as a result of the COVID health and economic pandemic, women lost more than one million more jobs than men by the end of 2020. Of this group, Black, Hispanic, and Asian women accounted for all of women's job losses in December, with 154,000 Black women dropping out of the labor force entirely.

We are facing some hellacious problems in the United States today. My hope and prayer is that we focus our collective attention on the women who are being left behind. President Biden, I supported your candidacy because you wanted someone like Vice President Harris to be the last person in the room when big decisions are made. My prayer is that all our leaders in Washington adequately serve the countless women who have put their all on the altars of sacrifice and have nothing left.

LETTER 5 (RAMBACHAN): "UNTRUTH NEVER SERVES JUSTICE AND THE COMMON GOOD." LETTER 69 (NGWA): "MOVE YOUR AGENDA BEYOND REPAIRING OUR NATION, TO REDESIGNING IT TOWARD JUSTICE AND EQUITY." LETTER 71 (Z. KASSAM): "IN THE ISLAMIC TRADITION, JUSTICE AND COMPASSION GO HAND IN HAND."

RELIGIOUS VOICES: DAYS 71–80

LETTER 71 | MARCH 31, 2021

Zayn Kassam

John Knox McLean Professor of Religious Studies, Pomona College

LETTER 72 | APRIL 1, 2021

David Fox Sandmel

Senior Advisor on Interreligious Affairs, ADL (Anti-Defamation League)

LETTER 73 | APRIL 2, 2021

Love L. Sechrest

Vice President for Academic Affairs and Associate Professor of New Testament, Columbia Theological Seminary

LETTER 74 | APRIL 3, 2021

Mai-Anh Le Tran

Vice President for Academic Affairs, Academic Dean, Associate Professor of Religious Education and Practical Theology, Garrett-Evangelical Theological Seminary

LETTER 75 | APRIL 4, 2021

Deirdre Good

Faculty, Stevenson School of Ministry, Diocese of Central Pennsylvania

LETTER 76 | APRIL 5, 2021

Aristotle Papanikolaou

Professor of Theology, Archbishop Demetrios Chair in Orthodox Theology and Culture, Fordham University

LETTER 77 | APRIL 6, 2021

Erica M. Ramirez

Director of Applied Research, Auburn Seminary

LETTER 78 | APRIL 7, 2021

Nicholas A. Grier

Assistant Professor of Practical Theology, Spiritual Care, and Counseling, Claremont School of Theology

LETTER 79 | APRIL 8, 2021

Ellen M. Ross

Howard M. and Charles F. Jenkins Professor of Quakerism and Peace Studies, Swarthmore College

LETTER 80 | APRIL 9, 2021

Amy Easton-Flake

Associate Professor of Ancient Scripture, Brigham Young University

Dear President Biden, Vice President Harris, and Members of the 117th Congress,

In the Islamic tradition, justice and compassion go hand in hand. *Raḥmah*, the word for compassion, understood interchangeably with mercy, stands out as one of the key attributes of God. Muslims begin their daily prayers with the phrase: "In the name of God, the Compassionate, the Merciful (*bismillāh ar-raḥmān ar-raḥīm*)."

The word for compassion derives from the Arabic root *r-ḥ-m*, which has the connotation of a womb (*ar-raḥm*), a place of nurturance and safety. What does compassion have to do with politics and governance? The Dalai Lama teaches: "Love and compassion are necessities, not luxuries. Without them, humanity cannot survive."

Compassion is needed to fulfill the vision of the Preamble to the U.S. Constitution: "establish Justice, insure domestic Tranquility, provide for the common defense, promote the general Welfare, and secure the Blessings of liberty to ourselves and our posterity…"

How can we "establish justice" without compassion for those who have been wronged, but also for those whose wrongdoing is rooted in the trauma of poverty, racism, and discrimination?

How can we "insure domestic tranquility" if we fail to see with the eyes of compassion that hunger, homelessness, illness, and unemployment result from our vast inequities of wealth, which also drive migrants to our borders?

How can we "provide for the common defense" with compassion for those who bear the costs of war, while refocusing some defense spending to foster peace and resolve conflicts before they escalate into war?

How can we "promote the general welfare" given the global threat posed by climate change? How might compassion for climate refugees, sinking nations, and mounting species loss intensify our investment in renewable forms of energy and actively engage us in global protocols for environmental sustainability?

How can we "secure the blessings of liberty to ourselves and our posterity" without compassion for one another and an embrace of the differences of race, ethnicity, religion, ability, gender, and economic station that make up the rich American tapestry and enrich us as members of the larger human family?

Let us take our cue from God, who says in the Qur'an: "My compassion (*raḥmah*) embraces all things" (7:156).

DAY 72, LETTER 72

David Fox Sandmel

Dear President Biden, Vice President Harris, and Members of the 117th Congress,

The prophet Zechariah, describing his vision of a restored society, tells the people: "These are the things you are to do: Speak the truth to one another, render true and perfect justice in your gates" (Zechariah 8:16). The psalmist considered truth and justice synonymous and imagined that together they form an essential connection between heaven and earth:

> *Today we are called by truth and justice to craft a new national narrative...*

"Faithfulness and truth meet;
justice and well-being kiss.
Truth springs up from the earth;
justice looks down from heaven." (Psalm 85:11–12)

And yet truth has been under attack in our nation. These attacks have endangered our health, resulted in violence, and further eroded the sense of commonality and trust in one another that is the foundation of a stable, functional society.

Moreover, we as a nation are being challenged to acknowledge some truths that have been denied for too long, the denial of which has resulted in innumerable injustices. The legacy of racism and bigotry in all its forms, blatant and hidden, continues to do irreparable harm, first and foremost to its immediate victims, but ultimately to us as a country and a society, morally and even economically.

Today we are called by truth and justice to craft a new national narrative that tells the whole truth. We seek a narrative that includes everyone, acknowledges our failures, and celebrates our successes. We need a new narrative to empower us to realize a shared understanding of justice in our national life.

Zechariah urged us to "speak the truth *to one another*." Speaking truth that leads to justice is a dialogic process; it requires each of us to engage with our neighbors in a manner that leads to mutual understanding, empathy, and ultimately to personal and national transformation.

Zechariah also spoke of rendering "true and perfect justice *in your gates*," referring to the responsibility of leadership to govern in that same spirit. We look to you to lead us toward a future of truth and justice, equality and equity, so that—in a phrase from the prophet Micah, beloved by George Washington—"all can sit under their vine and under their fig tree, with nothing to make them afraid" (Micah 4:4).

DAY 73, LETTER 73

Love L. Sechrest

Dear President Biden, Vice President Harris, and Members of the 117th Congress,

James Baldwin writes in *The Fire Next Time*: "Time catches up with kingdoms and crushes them, gets its teeth into doctrines and rends them … destroys doctrines by proving them to be untrue." Today I am looking for leaders who can unite a fractured nation and reject the realm of lies and false doctrines poisoning the body politic. It's easy to believe that we are running out of time as false narratives about who can have authority and who has the freedom to challenge or resist authority chip away at the heart of our democracy.

In the New Testament, the book of Ephesians speaks to the themes of unity and truth-telling. Ephesians 4:1–16 tells leaders to continue Christ's work of unifying the cosmos by tending to the divisions in their midst. Proclaiming that strangers and aliens are welcome in the household of God, Ephesians insists that leaders must speak the truth in love because we are in the same boat together (4:15, 25). Ephesians tells us that leaders are supplied by Christ to act as ligaments that bind the body politic together during stormy times (4:7–16).

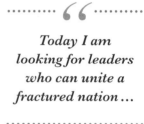

Today I am looking for leaders who can unite a fractured nation …

Today, if we are to make our way back from hate crimes, an insurrection, and the politics of grievance, then reconciliation must go hand in hand with truth telling and unity-preserving structures. This means telling the truth that our multiracial democracy is a recent, beautiful, and fragile thing, held together by organizers from Black, Indigenous, Latinx, Asian, and white communities. This means telling the truth that devotion to the filibuster for the sake of comity in the Senate is the height of privilege when democracy itself is at stake. This means Congress must pass and the president must sign legislation to protect access to the ballot for all Americans. We must not dishonor the sacrifices of those who fought to secure, mobilize, and exercise the right to vote in the face of overwhelming forces.

If, try as you may, you can't heal the deep divisions in our society, I pray that you will hold on to what is fragile and strengthen the structures that bind us together in keeping with the leadership vision of Ephesians.

Dear President Biden, Vice President Harris, and Members of the 117th Congress,

Of the many things the COVID-19 pandemic has made real and surreal, it is that we can be simultaneously terrorized and amazed, that life can be at once awful and awesome.

The inauguration of two lifelong public servants to the nation's highest offices, and the sight of a first Black/Asian American woman vice president, were for many emblematic of the United States in its most dignified instantiation. It was a re-presentation of the noblest forms of the "American idea" of which President Biden spoke: collective courage, conviction, conscience, collaboration. However, just two weeks before, we witnessed a terrifying display of deep-rooted white supremacist sedition, anarchy, and cowardice—a stark reminder that our country still cannot imagine the possibility of common futures and a common good *for all*.

> " *The world is in need of repair, and … its brokenness is repairable …*

The Biden administration has demonstrated hawkeyed attention to the critical issues of our lifetime: the raging COVID-19 pandemic, the choking economic crisis, the inertia of racial inequity and injustice, and the perils of climate change that threaten our very existence. These matters will take more than 100 days of executive orders. They require the unflinching resolve and principled actions of a people and a planet.

The "battle for the soul of the nation," as the president put it, is not a fight between winners and losers out of which some may suffer mortal wounds. It might be more akin to what Christian biblical scholar Melanie Johnson-DeBaufre describes as "utopian social dreaming." It is not sleepy-eyed wishful thinking, but rather an "engaged, directed daytime vision," a daringness to "dream the world as it ought to be," as Toni Morrison advised the 1988 Sarah Lawrence College graduates. Utopian social dreamers are acutely attuned to what philosopher Elizabeth V. Spelman wrote long ago: the world is in need of repair, and we humans insist that its brokenness is repairable. Christians would add that God is steadily at work in the ongoing regeneration of this world; our human responsibility is to join in that work.

This is the very same terror and amazement of Easter that Christians celebrate worldwide. We are terrified by our own death-dealing brokenness, and yet we continue to be amazed by God's regenerative, resurrectional power.

May this good news sustain and embolden you for the long and hard work ahead.

DAY 75, LETTER 75   **Deirdre Good**

Dear President Biden, Vice President Harris, and Members of the 117th Congress,

During the Second World War, in September 1939, paintings from London's National Gallery were hidden in Welsh mines to keep them safe. Over time the public complained that some contemporary art and concerts were taking place in the National Gallery, but there were no great paintings to see. A patron pleaded: "Because London's face is scarred and bruised these days, we need more than ever to see beautiful things." After considerable deliberation, the trustees decided that one picture a month could be brought back from Wales and hang in the National Gallery, even at great risk. A poll was conducted, and the public selected Titian's *Noli me tangere* (Do Not Touch Me) as the overwhelming first choice.

Neil MacGregor, recent director of the National Gallery, speculates that what drew the public to Titian's painting within the context of nightly bombings and air raids on London was the encounter between the living and the dead. Titian depicts the moment when Mary Magdalene, having first noticed the gardener outside Jesus' tomb, hears him call her name: "Mariam." She replies: "*Rabboni*!" (which means "my Teacher") and reaches out towards the risen Christ. As he bends away, he leans over and blesses her (John 20:11–18).

Lent is the journey from death to life that culminates in Easter …

The painting investigates what happens to physical love after death, and how physical love and spiritual love meet—or do not meet—but still can be reconciled. MacGregor sees Titian's masterpiece as an incomparable meditation on love that continues without physical contact or proximity, for Christ protects, blesses, and loves without admitting physical touch. Enforced separation of sudden, unexpected death is overcome in a painting, showing connections between the living and the dead. As Song of Songs reminds us: "Love is strong as death" (8:6).

Lent is the journey from death to life that culminates in Easter when a community comes into being that holds out a promise of new and transformed life for the world. Let us enact that promise for all.

Aristotle Papanikolaou

Dear President Biden, Vice President Harris, and Members of the 117th Congress,

I write this letter during the fourth week of Orthodox Lent, a sacred time as we journey to the crucifixion, resurrection, and ascension of Jesus Christ. There are many fasting rules during Lent, and inasmuch as Lent presents an opportunity, it also presents a danger. Greater distance from God occurs not because we fail to follow the rules, but because we follow them in a way that treats our relationship with God and with others like a checklist.

This focus on the rules can obfuscate the real point of asceticism, which is a training toward a transformation of the heart: a heart that loves as God loves the world and all that is in it. That kind of love takes work and practice. That kind of love requires asceticism. It's not easy, yet it's possible. We can love as God loves. We can become god and be deified—this is the core of our belief in the Incarnate Christ: *theosis*.

> **We need a politics of love, of communion, of theosis.**

One may be prompted to ask, as another great observer of the human condition once did: "What's love got to do with it?" That is the great error in thinking about politics—that love has nothing to do with it. In our Orthodox tradition, ascetics went into the Egyptian desert to become closer to God. The political space is but one of many deserts in which we must resist the temptation to demonize the stranger and enemy. Especially in the field of politics, we are challenged to realize what is possible for human beings: to love the other, even the enemy and the stranger (Leviticus 19:33–34; Mark 12:31).

In a time of heightened demonization, in an era when so many hide behind the law to avoid responding to the demands of justice for the marginalized in our country, we need to think of a politics beyond the contractual, a possible politics that facilitates incarnating patterns of relationships where all are seen in their irreducible uniqueness. We need a politics of love, of communion, of *theosis*.

Dear President Biden, Vice President Harris, and Members of the 117th Congress,

Pundits, religious leaders, and scholars have framed January's Capitol riot as a vivid illustration of the risks posed by Christian nationalism. Wild-eyed zealots, desecrating the Capitol, together serve as Exhibit A of Christian nationalism's dangers.

Robert Jones' *White Too Long: The Legacy of White Supremacy in American Christianity* (2019) recounts how evangelicals, mainline Protestants, and Catholics have long helped to model and sacralize the United States' race hierarchy. After centuries of complicity in racist oppression, Jones surmises: "the norms of white supremacy have become deeply and broadly integrated into white Christian identity, operating far below the level of consciousness." As a result, to many, "Christianity and a cultural form of white supremacy now feel indistinguishable."

In such a context, we might magnify obvious examples, like the Capitol riot, in an attempt to make racist subterranean dynamics undeniable.

But if we look deeper, we could see that the inauguration of President Biden, too, proffered Christian nationalism. How else to explain Garth Brooks singing "Amazing Grace"—his baritone performance interspersed with images of the American flag? Two minutes in, Brooks asked everyone watching to join him, "united" in singing a Christian mainstay. Though masked, Jennifer Lopez, Lady Gaga, and Vice President Harris appeared to join in. Dressed in jeans, his cowboy hat poignantly removed, Brooks', in his performance, modeled that white Christianity can powerfully represent the nation, if white Christian men approach this role with virtuous humility.

> "
> *…our religious diversity is both a cause and measure of our flourishing.*

Such performances suggest that respectable, respectful Christian nationalism is welcome—even potentially necessary. But an America that is both multiracial and egalitarian will also need to be consciously, constructively pluralistic in faith. To this end, the Biden inauguration's interfaith prayer service was a start; as a nation, we need to go much further.

Any one faith tradition—when in power—can readily fall prey to the corruption of its highest aims. At Auburn Seminary, we actively embrace diverse religious traditions, in part, because we believe diverse witnesses sharpen our commitments to justice in the public square.

I invite you all to consider that part of your public service will need to include casting a vision for this nation in which our religious diversity is both a cause and measure of our flourishing.

Dear President Biden, Vice President Harris, and Members of the 117th Congress,

As I type this letter, the nation is re-membering the killing of George Floyd. The trial of Derek Chauvin is well underway. Clips of testimonies and newly released videos of Mr. Floyd's killing are flooding social media. This is only three and a half weeks after the killing of Asian Americans in the Atlanta spa shootings. Tragic. These events point to the reality that we still live in a country that does not acknowledge the humanity of Black and Asian people in the United States of America. Part of the problem is that the United States too often proceeds with "progress and innovation," while forgetting its Black, Brown, Indigenous, and Asian citizens. To live up to the best of our ideals and potential, we must re-member every person and community in the United States.

> *Re-membering is a gift that positions us to nurture justice, healing, and reconciliation.*

Re-membering involves living with an awareness of the past and making intentional efforts to include our fellow human beings as members of the American family. Re-membering requires us to do two things. First, we must never forget. We must remember constructively the events of our past. After 9/11, many declared that we would never forget. Yet, too often, the United States proceeds, forgetting its devastating history of enslaving, lynching, exploiting, and dehumanizing Black, Brown, Indigenous, and Asian people. Additionally, we must remember the contributions, cultures, and ancestors of Black, Brown, Indigenous, and Asian people. Secondly, re-membering means that we must include Black, Brown, Indigenous, and Asian people as members of the human family. Colonization, white supremacy, and all forms of domination and exploitation have caused many people to forget and exclude them from membership in the American family.

As we celebrate this Holy Season, I am reminded of the actions of Jesus, welcoming everyone to the table and inviting disciples to take Holy Communion in remembrance of him (Luke 22:19). To remember Jesus is to re-member the poor, marginalized, and oppressed. Re-membering is a gift that positions us to nurture justice, healing, and reconciliation.

I give thanks that you have taken the oath to serve the people of our country. May you re-member all citizens and communities of the United States of America and lead with bold empathy and compassion.

Dear President Biden, Vice President Harris, and Members of the 117th Congress,

What vision of peace guides you?

History demonstrates that the possibilities for peace may astonish us. The power of peace rooted in love can move mountains (Gospel of Thomas, Saying 48). I urge you to seek inspiration in stories and experiences from religiously grounded American social movements for peace.

Cutting-edge Quaker reformers from the seventeenth century to the present such as John Woolman, Anthony Benezet, and Lucretia Mott consistently invoke a transformative vision of a world where "nation shall not lift up sword against nation, nor shall they learn war anymore" (Isaiah 2:4). Committed to peace as a means and an end, these Quaker religious leaders challenge us to "discover how far we are implicated, individually and nationally," in war and the interlinked oppressions that make "the rich richer and the poor poorer" (Mott).

Cultures of peace are all around us if we turn our attention to them. The 20th-century Quaker sociologist Elise Boulding wrote about *Cultures of Peace: The Hidden Side of History* and the importance of intention in their creation: "The culture of peace … has to be learned." We are social beings, and yet each of us is unique, so we have to learn how to deal creatively, on both the personal and global scale, with our varied "mosaic of identities, attitudes, values, beliefs, and institutional patterns" (*Friends Journal* 46.9).

> " *Cultures of peace are all around us if we turn our attention to them.*

Mr. President, your own Roman Catholic tradition inspired prophetic peace builders such as Dorothy Day, Thomas Merton, and the Berrigan brothers. Today, the Kings Bay Plowshares 7 bear witness to the imminent threat nuclear weapons pose "to the Earth and life on earth," as well as the weapons' role in perpetuating economic and racial injustice and the global climate crisis. These Plowshares activists belong to a lineage of peace builders who show another way: human interconnectedness and a vision of "what it looks like to be a disciple of Christ in the 21st century."

I appeal to you all to lend your support to peace research and study, educational programs, peace museums, storytellers, mediators, diplomats, and negotiators with time-tested commitments to nonviolent conflict resolution. May the vision of a just and peaceful world inspire you to lead with courage and imagination.

Dear President Biden, Vice President Harris, and Members of the 117th Congress,

Much of the future is determined by the nature of our perspective and consequential acts. The current state of the world is a marvel of previously unbelievable advancements, with wonderful and inspiring opportunities at every turn. At the same time, there are long-existent security, stability, sustainability, and systemic issues that you must address. I hope you will use your positions of power to help Americans gain a crucial perspective shift on how we view and interact with one another.

That perspective shift should come from the foundational teaching of many of our faith traditions: We are all co-equals before God, and God has guided us to love and care for each other as siblings. Our common humanity is not defined or limited by borders, race, gender, ethnicity, socioeconomics, political affiliations, or nations.

The women of Exodus show what crossing entrenched identity divisions makes possible. The story of the Exodus unfolds because Shiphrah and Puah, midwives to the Hebrews whose ethnicity and nationality are notably ambiguous, make an independent moral decision to defy Pharaoh's order to kill all the male babies (Exodus 1:15–21). Later, Pharaoh's daughter follows her emotional, ethical impulse and chooses to work in concert with Hebrew women in an act of cross-gender, cross-class, cross-ethnic, and cross-national deliverance to save Moses' life (2:5–10). Eventually, the Egyptian women cross ethnic, class, and national lines to aid the Hebrew women as they flee into the wilderness by providing them with material goods (3:22; 12:35).

> *The women of Exodus show what crossing entrenched identity divisions makes possible.*

These biblical women illustrate the profound influence of individual actions and the necessity of forming cooperative networks. Their examples underscore how we must extend compassion across national borders. So while you seek to eradicate partisan divisions, profound social inequalities, and systemic racism, classism, and sexism within the United States, I pray you will extend that same level of concern to every individual on planet Earth. Avoid war with all possible efforts and provide aid, assistance, and outreach in abundance. Lead by example as you seek to help all Americans recognize our shared humanity and co-dependency with all the inhabitants of the world—knowing that we do in actuality uplift ourselves when we uplift others.

LETTER 14. Díaz
"Gift every American with leadership that models our democratic ideals, enables **healing**, and protects us from all enemies, foreign and domestic."

LETTER 46. Jones
"We need your calming, feeding, **healing** actions at this moment in time more than we need anything else."

LETTER 19. Carvalho
"...you have taken up this near-impossible task of bringing **healing** and reconciliation while also leading the nation forward using your own moral compass."

HEALING

LETTER 53. Khalsa-Baker
"This transformation requires a change of heart, mind, and action to **heal** old wounds, serve one another, and protect the dignity of all life."

LETTER 24. Hussain
"With justice, and in faith, we need to right our wrongs and **heal** our nation."

LETTER 78. Grier
"Re-membering is a gift that positions us to nurture justice, **healing**, and reconciliation."

RELIGIOUS VOICES: DAYS 81–90

LETTER 81 | APRIL 10, 2021

Efraín Agosto

Professor of New Testament Studies,
New York Theological Seminary

LETTER 82 | APRIL 11, 2021

Jaime Clark-Soles

Professor of New Testament and
Altshuler Distinguished Teaching Professor,
Perkins School of Theology, SMU

LETTER 83 | APRIL 12, 2021

Tazim R. Kassam

Associate Professor of Religion,
Syracuse University

LETTER 84 | APRIL 13, 2021

Shreena Niketa Gandhi

Fixed Term Assistant Professor of
Religious Studies, College of Arts and
Letters, Michigan State University

LETTER 85 | APRIL 14, 2021

Christopher Key Chapple

Doshi Professor of Indic and Comparative
Theology, Loyola Marymount University

LETTER 86 | APRIL 15, 2021

Brian Rainey

Lecturer in Biblical Studies, Princeton
Theological Seminary

LETTER 87 | APRIL 16, 2021

Bryan N. Massingale

James and Nancy Buckman Chair in
Applied Christian Ethics,
Fordham University

LETTER 88 | APRIL 17, 2021

Anna C. Miller

Associate Professor of New Testament
and Early Christianity, Xavier University

LETTER 89 | APRIL 18, 2021

Nikky-Guninder Kaur Singh

Crawford Professor and Chair of
Religious Studies, Colby College

LETTER 90 | APRIL 19, 2021

Shively T. J. Smith

Assistant Professor of New Testament,
Boston University School of Theology

Dear President Biden, Vice President Harris, and Members of the 117th Congress,

February 2021 marked the 70th anniversary since my father, Efraín Agosto, Sr., left his birthplace, the Island of Puerto Rico, seeking work in New York City. He was part of a major wave of Puerto Ricans that left the Island in the post–World War II period. By summertime, after he had found a job and a place to live, my mother, Emerita Agosto Perez, joined him. My sisters and I have been able to forge successful professional and personal lives thanks to the sacrifices of our parents.

As we look toward the southern border today, where other families seek relief from social and economic crises in their home countries, I am hopeful for a renewed effort on the part of your administration to do better for them. The previous administration refused to do better, instead exacerbating the situation with inhumane policies of family separation and abrogation of international refugee laws and practices. We can do better, even as some congressional forces resist change and refuse to acknowledge the historic contributions of immigrants to the social and economic fabric of our nation.

> *…serve with compassion and excellence those who suffer around the world.*

To enact better immigration policy, we must *think* deeper. As the New Testament writer, the Apostle Paul, insisted: "Finally, beloved, whatever is true, whatever is honorable, whatever is just, whatever is pure, whatever is pleasing, whatever is commendable, if there is any *excellence* and if there is anything worthy of praise, *think* about these things" (Philippians 4:8). Would that your administration and members of Congress *think* long and hard, putting aside partisan differences and xenophobia to arrive at fair, honorable, and just actions on behalf of the suffering families coming to the border seeking solace and justice, life and well-being.

We have the resources and values in this nation, even amid a pandemic, to serve with compassion and excellence those who suffer around the world, including our nearest neighbors. They in turn will help us build better. My parents thought so and did so. We should too.

Thank you for thinking deeply and justly in this fateful season and working tirelessly toward excellence in government service.

Jaime Clark-Soles

Dear President Biden, Vice President Harris, and Members of the 117th Congress,

In John 11:1–44, Mary and Martha summon Jesus when their brother Lazarus becomes gravely ill. By the time Jesus arrives, Lazarus is dead, the mourners are wailing, the sisters are mired in the "if-only" game, and all hope for death to be overcome has been lost or shoved into the distant future.

Likewise, you have inherited a nation marked by death, wailing, "if-only," and tattered hope. Against all odds, Lazarus' story ends with resurrection and life in the here and now. Will America's?

In this story, Jesus moves people from death to life. How?

He shows up. He doesn't just witness their grief, he *enters* it: "Jesus wept" (11:35). He accompanies them to the site of their devastation and actively listens to the raw-throated voices of the ones actually experiencing the suffering firsthand. He leads them to "roll away the stone" and face a difficult truth: there is a stench (11:39).

> **He doesn't just witness their grief, he enters it …**

As you've begun to do already, may you continue to show up, listen to, and weep with our aggrieved siblings who suffer most from racism, ableism, heterosexism, and other death-dealing forces.

By the (infinite) power invested in him, Jesus raises Lazarus. But when Lazarus exits the tomb, he is still bound. He is alive, but not yet free. It may seem strange that Jesus commands the *community*: "Unbind him and let him go" (11:44), for Jesus could have done that himself. The lesson for us is clear: if we're going to be an America where all are truly free, together we must be willing to remove the death wrappings with our own hands.

By the (finite) power invested in you, lead us from death to life. Show up. Weep with us. Be frank about the stench, lest we lose our sense of smell. Take life-giving action. Enlist our help.

Astonishingly, after Jesus raises Lazarus, he declares that we will do even greater works than he did (John 14:12). I believe him, and I hope you do too. Leaving behind "if-onlys" about the past and clichéd wishes for the future, we can accomplish these works here and now. Lead on.

DAY 83, LETTER 83

Tazim R. Kassam

Dear President Biden, Vice President Harris, and Members of the 117th Congress,

Engraved on coins in the United States is the script, *E pluribus unum* ("Out of many, one"). Given the present state of affairs in the nation, this motto remains an aspiration. The many have not come together as one greater than its parts. America is disunited and fragmented by difference; instead of being a source of strength, diversity has become a cause for weakness.

When John Adams, Benjamin Franklin, and Thomas Jefferson proposed the motto for the first Great Seal of the United States in 1776, they had in mind uniting many states under one nation; but *E pluribus unum* can be a vision equally praiseworthy for a country of immigrants from around the world.

We have come to see our differences as defining us against each other, rather than as an opportunity to celebrate the unique threads and colors we contribute to the tapestry of humanity. When unity is mistaken to mean uniformity, conformity, and normativity, every kind of diversity becomes cause for distrust and division.

> **Pluralism and the merits of diversity must be taught.**

The following verse from the Qur'an aptly captures the appreciation of diversity and value placed on learning about each other: "O humanity! We created you of a male and female and *made you peoples and tribes that you may know each other.* Indeed, the noblest of you in the sight of God is the most righteous in conduct. Verily, God is Omniscient and All-knowing" (49:13).

Tribalism, which is based on blood and ethnocentricity, is a more natural state of human society than pluralism. Pluralism and the merits of diversity must be taught. A wellspring of knowledge is required for there to be mutual recognition, enlightened interaction, and social inclusion.

Unfortunately, education in the U.S. provides little exposure to the many cultures within its borders and around the world. The result is distrust and antagonism, often expressed through violence. Misguided suspicions reveal the gulf of ignorance that divides citizens into factions.

We need to reform our educational system by integrating a pluralist worldview into the curriculum. Investing in a fruitful conversation between cultures through the creative and performing arts of our global traditions of music, dance, poetry, storytelling, and visual arts is one way to actualize the motto, "out of many, one."

DAY 84, LETTER 84

Shreena Niketa Gandhi

Dear President Biden, Vice President Harris, and Members of the 117th Congress,

If our American values motivate us to try to eradicate discrimination, then we need to listen to the voices of those who are being discriminated against. In the South Asian community, that means listening to the voices and stories of Dalits, a community considered to be at the "bottom" of or outside the Hindu caste system.

Like other immigrants, Dalits come to America expecting that anyone can achieve anything in the United States. But this myth of meritocracy overlooks the structural advantages that many South Asian immigrants arrive with, like a degree. The myth of meritocracy also ignores that many South Asian immigrants come with another privilege: caste.

While all too many South Asians in this country experience various forms of racism, many also perpetuate another form of oppression connected to casteism. A 2016 survey by Equality Labs, a Dalit civil rights organization, found that many Dalits experience discrimination from non-Dalit South Asians in the United States. Investigating a recent case of harassment in the workplace at Cisco, Yashica Dutt found that people "feared that revealing their identity as a Dalit working in the American tech industry filled with higher-caste Indians would ruin their career."

> *...encourage us to be as passionate about caste discrimination as many of us are about racism and sexism.*

Because caste is an inextricable part of South Asian culture—particularly Hinduism—caste travels with South Asian immigrants, just like our languages, foods, and religions. Many Hindus in the U.S. and India say they do not see caste, like many white people in the U.S. say they do not see race. Yet it is undeniable that shruti and smriti scriptures reify the caste structure, just as many Hindu rituals and celebrations, such as Holi, do the same.

Vice President Harris, you often talk about your inspirational mother, Shyamala Gopalan Harris. Remember that being a Brahmin gave her certain advantages, including her ability to travel to the U.S. to further her education. Acknowledging caste privilege does not take away from anyone's achievements; rather, it helps to contextualize them.

As you engage with South Asians, encourage us to be as passionate about caste discrimination as many of us are about racism and sexism. We are counting on your leadership, openness, and honesty to help us address the caste system and its ramifications for us as Americans.

DAY 85, LETTER 85

Dear President Biden, Vice President Harris, and Members of the 117th Congress,

Our country, like the rest of the world, has experienced turmoil during the past year: worry, stress, and distress over health, politics, and overall issues of fairness. So much trouble on so many fronts is taking a serious toll on our collective well-being.

Many millions of Americans practice Yoga regularly to cultivate mental, emotional, and physical health. Though some think of Yoga as a fad, it actually has a long history. Yoga originated in Asia and has been part of many faith traditions: Hindu, Jain, Buddhist, Sikh, Muslim, and Taoist. Millions of Christians, Jews, and people of no faith at all now practice Yoga as well.

Mahatma Gandhi employed two core precepts of Yoga to free India from British colonial rule: nonviolence (*ahimsa*) and holding always to truth (*satyagraha*). His nonviolent protests helped inspire the American civil rights movement.

Like many young people, I took up the daily practice as a teenager in the 1970s. I studied with Gurani Anjali Inti, an immigrant to the United States who grew up in Calcutta (now Kolkata). She taught people from all walks of life and all faiths. Her teachings included weekly reflections on how to cultivate the good life through the practices of nonviolence, truthfulness, cheerfulness, deep breathing, and daily performance of Yoga postures. We also learned how to meditate on the bounties of nature, connecting with the great elements of earth, water, fire, and air, all contained within space.

> " *Returning to the body and breath allows the renewal of the spirit ...*

Yoga can be effective for addressing the pressing problems that confront people of all ages, but particularly the young: stress, depression, and anxiety. This low-cost tool fosters a sense of well-being and a sense of purpose. It provides a much-needed antidote to a life too often defined by the trivialities of shopping and social media. Returning to the body and breath allows the renewal of the spirit, essential for personal and societal health.

Michelle Obama brought Yoga to the White House lawn. Hopefully, this tradition will be revived—not only in the White House, but also in the House and Senate.

DAY 86, LETTER 86

Dear President Biden, Vice President Harris, and Members of the 117th Congress,

While reflecting on all of the crisis and turmoil over the last year, I have repeatedly come back to the word "apocalypse." "Apocalypse" literally means an uncovering or unveiling, not necessarily the end of the world. Apocalyptic texts in the Bible give readers a peek at the powerful, and often terrifying, forces at work behind a society's curtain of complacency and collective denial—also known as "business as usual."

These powerful forces can be symbolized by grotesque beasts with multiple heads, extraordinary natural disasters, or even stars falling from the skies (Daniel 7; Matthew 24:3–31; Revelation 6; 8:7–9:21; 11:7; 12–13; 16). The imagery is supposed to shake readers out of their complacency and force them to respect the awesome powers—both good and evil—that operate behind the curtain. And the apocalypse genre uses horror to convey the urgency of the moment.

Over the last year, we watched much horror unfold: the brutal killing of George Floyd, police repression of Black Lives Matter protesters, the pandemic, the economic crisis, the inhumane treatment of asylum seekers, the human exacerbation of natural disasters seen in the Texas winter storms, and the insurrection on January 6.

> *Our apocalypse has revealed some awful beasts.*

These are apocalyptic events that uncover and expose powerful, terrifying truths about the U.S. They unmask the white supremacy woven into the fabric of the nation—and the kid gloves with which it has been treated. They unveil the authoritarian motives of many politicians and religious groups. They uncover the disrespect that our socioeconomic way of life shows toward Creation. They expose the contempt many business leaders and their political enablers have for ordinary people. They reveal the effects of unjust foreign policy toward Central America. And they demonstrate the crude selfishness encouraged by the American myths of rugged individualism and exceptionalism.

All of these problems existed before now; but our national apocalypse has thrown them in our faces in a way we are not used to. This is not the time to tinker around with policy. It is not the time for posturing or pandering. It is time for bold action. Our apocalypse has revealed some awful beasts. I pray you take its message of urgency seriously.

Dear President Biden, Vice President Harris, and Members of the 117th Congress,

I write this letter as we approach the end of this administration's first 100 days. My mind turns to a fundamental conviction shared by many religious traditions and people of goodwill, namely, the importance of truth. Some follow Jesus' invitation that "the truth will set you free" (John 8:32). Others heed the Ten Commandments and the admonition against bearing false witness against one's neighbor (Exodus 20:16). But all agree that truth is an essential foundation for social life.

There is much talk today about the "Big Lie"—the false belief that the 2020 election was illegitimate—and its effects on our national life. But that's not the Big Lie. The Big Lie in American life is that those who don't look like us, talk like us, think like us, pray like us, or love like us are not worthy. Not equal. Not human. It's the lie that those who are not like us don't belong and aren't truly American—especially those with darker skin.

This is the lie that unites the rise in virulent anti-Semitism; the disparate impact of the COVID pandemic upon communities of color; the murders of George Floyd, Breonna Taylor, Ahmaud Arbery, and so many others; the manifold increase in anti-Asian violence; the tragic inhumanity at our southern border; the spate of restrictive voter legislation; and the insurrection at the Capitol. These are not isolated realities. They are rooted in the Big Lie that those who are not white and Christian are not equally human.

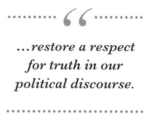

...restore a respect for truth in our political discourse.

That lie jeopardizes the survival of our democracy. We cannot enjoy social peace in a culture of lies, falsehoods, and evasions of truth.

Truth matters. This conviction was powerfully articulated by Pope John Paul II, who declared: "Truth is the basis, foundation, and mother of justice" ("Address to the Roman Rota," 1980). Without a respect for truth and dedication to the truth of the equal sacred dignity and worth of every human being, life together is endangered, compromised, even impossible.

As you lead our country, I implore you to restore a respect for truth in our political discourse. Only a renewed dedication to truth can lead us beyond our current impasses and heal the soul of a wounded and divided nation.

Anna C. Miller

Dear President Biden, Vice President Harris, and Members of the 117th Congress,

It has been an interminable four years for many who believe not only in democracy, but in the humanity and full citizenship of women, people of color, and those in the LGBTQ community. How do we move forward when it feels as if those beliefs were under constant attack? Can we heal as a nation when work still progresses to deny votes to groups whose citizenship—whose very humanity—has been contested too many times in this "land of the free"? Certainly, our government and national leaders must play a critical role in reasserting democratic norms, decency, and compassion. However, we also need communal processes for our citizenry that can lead us toward a hopeful future.

When I sat down to think of what parts of the biblical tradition might have something to offer us at this moment, the word that came into my mind was "covenant." In the Hebrew Bible, the Israelites enter into binding covenants with the creator God who has special concern for the marginalized. In perhaps the most dramatic example, the people stand at Mount Sinai after their deliverance from Egyptian slavery and commit to a relationship with God and with each other (Exodus 19–20). God tells this covenant community that they must make justice for the poor, widows, orphans, and the stranger, remembering that "you were a slave in Egypt and the Lord your God redeemed you from there" (Deuteronomy 24:17–18).

> **In this country, the times demand our own covenant renewal.**

In this country, the times demand our own covenant renewal. As communities, we must find ways to reaffirm what Cornell West calls our American civil religion: "that complex web of religious ideals of deliverance and salvation and political ideals of freedom, democracy and equality." Collectively, we need to remember that all people are created equal and that every citizen must have the same rights to freedom, security, and political participation.

I pray that our citizens and you, our elected officials, will come together in the next four years for "Sinai moments" in which we reaffirm democracy and our communal bonds. During those moments, I hope we can register the humanity in each face within our diverse communities. Remembering the gifts many of us have received, may we go forward, prepared to work for justice.

DAY 89, LETTER 89

Nikky-Guninder Kaur Singh

Dear President Biden, Vice President Harris, and Members of the 117th Congress,

Amidst this season of new beginnings in nature and the religious calendars of many faiths, it is reassuring to have you at the helm of our nation.

Attracted by Disneyland and American education, I came to the U.S. as a teenager from India. I thrived in this new world, the land of liberty and equality. It was here that I discovered my Sikh heritage and my passion for Sikh literature and art, which I am fortunate to share with my wonderful students at Colby College.

> *May we ... enjoy arabesques of mutuality and love.*

But in the last four years, American democracy and decency were undermined; truth and knowledge were abandoned by many, even in the highest echelons of power. Education is about knowledge, and religion is about truth—and both of these pillars of American society were threatened. For many, this has been a time of terrible anxiety, confusion, and dangerous polarization. With a new administration, many are starting to feel comfort and relief.

At this time of transition and new beginnings, the Sikh sacred text *Guru Granth* can inspire us:

To imagine the one infinite reality (*ikk aon kar*). This is the same one thread on which each of us with our unique light is beaded.

To live perpetually alive to this One in our actions (*karam kamae*). This is "love in action," the maxim of civil rights leader John Lewis.

To speak and hear the language of infinite love (*bhakhia bhau apar*). This is the "radical empathy" championed by Pulitzer Prize winner Isabel Wilkerson.

To rejoice in the wondrous plurality of the world. This is the idea that there is only One Being, "and yet, marvel of marvels, no two entities are alike" (*koe na kis hi jaisa*).

President Biden, we at Colby were profoundly touched by your passion and compassion when you visited us in 2017. We are confident that under your leadership, we will be able to get rid of toxic hate. May we plant flowers for a public park where we can come together with all our ideological differences, our diverse complexions, genders, and sexualities, and enjoy arabesques of mutuality and love.

Shively T. J. Smith

Dear President Biden, Vice President Harris, and Members of the 117th Congress,

At the end of his autobiography, *With Head and Heart,* Howard Thurman declared: "I take my stand for the future and for the generations who follow over the bridges we already have crossed. It is here that the meaning of the hunger of the heart is unified. The Head and the Heart at last inseparable … " I offer this quotation as encouragement. Cultivate the habit of stilling yourself to ponder: what bridges am I building and crossing for future generations today?

Howard Thurman was a mentor to Rev. Dr. Martin Luther King Jr. and became the first African American dean of a predominantly white university: my own institution, Boston University (1953–1965). He believed that bridge-building and bridge-crossing are deepened through intentional dialogue between diverse heads, hearts, and hands. Unified in collaboration, not uniformity, diverse communities can build, cross, and stand for the flourishing of all God's creation.

No matter the fear or resistance before you, I hope you commit to Thurman's principles. To encourage such reflection, I offer my meditation, inspired by his autobiography, called "Bridge Crossings":

> We take our "stand for the future and for the generations who follow …"
> We cross our bridges so they will have bridges to cross.
> Not everyone will construct the bridges we know must be built;
> but we build them anyway.
> Not everyone will travel across the bridges we know must be crossed;
> but we travel across them anyway.
> Sometimes we will have to brace ourselves for the backlash,
> which waits patiently for us to cross over.
> But like John Lewis and the 600 marchers
> crossing the Edmund Pettus Bridge to stand for the voting rights
> of African Americans and *all* American citizens,
> we must travel to the other side, nonetheless.

I hope your resolve to create bridge crossings deepens, so that future generations cross our bridges, extending and reinforcing them as they travel, while charting their own bridge-building projects.

FREEDOM

LETTER 88 | A. MILLER: "Collectively, we need to remember that all people are created equal and that every citizen must have the same rights to **freedom**, security, and political participation."

FREEDOM

LETTER 43 | KOOSED: "...reproductive justice is a matter of religious **freedom**, and true **freedom** of religion means allowing different people to make different decisions in conversation with their own religious traditions."

FREEDOM

LETTER 73 | SECHREST: "It's easy to believe that we are running out of time as false narratives about who can have authority and who has the **freedom** to challenge or resist authority chip away at the heart of our democracy."

FREEDOM

RELIGIOUS VOICES: DAYS 91–100

LETTER 91 | APRIL 20, 2021

Andrew Rehfeld

President, Hebrew Union College – Jewish Institute of Religion

LETTER 92 | APRIL 21, 2021

Varun Soni

Dean of Religious and Spiritual Life, University of Southern California

LETTER 93 | APRIL 22, 2021

Dawn M. Nothwehr

Erica and Harry John Family Endowed Chair in Catholic Theological Ethics, Catholic Theological Union-Chicago

LETTER 94 | APRIL 23, 2021

Raj Nadella

Samuel A. Cartledge Associate Professor of New Testament, Columbia Theological Seminary

LETTER 95 | APRIL 24, 2021

Kelly Brown Douglas

Dean, Bill and Judith Moyers Chair in Theology, Episcopal Divinity School at Union Theological Seminary in the City of New York

LETTER 96 | APRIL 25, 2021

Santiago Slabodsky

Robert and Florence Kaufman Endowed Chair in Jewish Studies and Associate Professor of Religion, Hofstra University

LETTER 97 | APRIL 26, 2021

Hamza M. Zafer

Associate Professor of Near Eastern Languages and Civilization, University of Washington

LETTER 98 | APRIL 27, 2021

Homayra Ziad

Director, Program in Islamic Studies, Johns Hopkins University

LETTER 99 | APRIL 28, 2021

Gay L. Byron

Professor of New Testament, Howard University School of Divinity

LETTER 100 | APRIL 29, 2021

Daniel Fisher-Livne

Assistant Professor of Bible, Hebrew Union College – Jewish Institute of Religion

Andrew Rehfeld

Dear President Biden, Vice President Harris, and Members of the 117th Congress,

As you start governing our great nation, you might be inclined to look to our sacred texts for inspiration—and for good reason. Like the most important political speeches in history, these texts inspire us to seek justice and pursue the common good. As you now move from campaigning to governing, these lofty ideals become grounded in the more mundane.

In the Jewish tradition, we believe that sacred routines—seemingly mundane daily practices and habits—are essential to achieving our highest aspirations. We oblige ourselves to giving *tzedakah* (charity), even when we hardly have enough for ourselves. We study, pray, visit the sick, or perform other acts of *hesed* (generosity and kindness), even if we don't feel we have the time or energy. Over time, the discipline of these routine habits shapes our character for the better, thereby giving our days a deeper sense of meaning and purpose. As "one good deed leads to another" (*mitzvah goreret mitzvah*) (Pirke Avot 4:2), our self-interest becomes aligned with a more universal pursuit of justice and the common good.

> **Over time,
> the discipline of
> these routine habits
> shapes our character
> for the better ...**

In the U.S., the Rule of Law serves a similar purpose. It constrains the arbitrary rule of those in power, ensuring the discipline to honor the process of lawmaking rather than glorify the lawmakers themselves. Individuals and institutions are obliged to follow the Rule of Law no matter their self-interests or desires, thereby limiting the ability to abuse their power.

It is no coincidence that the Constitution, the holiest of American documents, is filled with mundane rules and is rather short on inspirational text. Its virtue is to provide the building blocks and processes to limit injustices and inspire us to strive towards the values of equity, righteousness, justice, and freedom that define and unite us as a nation.

So be not discouraged that the rhetoric of the campaign now gives way to the reality of governing. May your ingrained habits of striving toward the Good, the Right, and the Just give you resilience and resolve as you work to attain your highest aspirations and bring about a brighter future for our nation and our world.

DAY 92, LETTER 92

Varun Soni

Dear President Biden, Vice President Harris, and Members of the 117th Congress,

In all of the world's sacred texts, there are powerful narratives of natural disasters and disease—from floods to plagues—that test humanity. Each moment of struggle and tragedy that emerges from these challenges offers an opportunity for renewal, rebirth, and redemption.

Over the course of the last year, we have collectively faced apocalyptic scenarios of biblical proportions: a global pandemic, civil unrest, political instability, fires and floods, and even a massive swarm of locusts! And while everyone is eagerly anticipating a return to normalcy, we will never go back to the way things were, nor should that be our aspiration. Like previous generations, we have been given a once-in-a-century opportunity to reimagine our world anew.

Moving forward, my hope and prayer is that as human beings we will fundamentally change our relationship with animals. Over the course of my lifetime, many of the significant infectious diseases that have plagued us—HIV/AIDS, SARS, Ebola, and now COVID-19—were caused by the abuse of animals. And we also know that one of the largest contributing factors to catastrophic climate change is factory farming and the wholesale slaughtering of animals for human consumption. If we truly care about preventing the next infectious disease, and if we are really going to address the civilizational threat of catastrophic climate change, then we must act boldly and bravely, with inspired leadership and the strength of our conviction.

> *… we have been given a once-in-a-century opportunity to reimagine our world anew.*

My Hindu faith teaches me that all sentient beings—including animals—have a soul, and that the soul is a reflection of the divine. That is why many Hindu deities are depicted in animal form, and why many Hindus do not consume meat. As Hindus, we believe that the Earth is a manifestation of the Goddess (*Devi*); as human beings, our duty (*dharma*) is to protect the natural world by living and breathing nonviolence (*ahimsa*).

I implore you, as leaders of the most powerful nation in human history, to reconsider the policies that contribute to the abuse of animals and the destruction of our planet. Our very survival depends upon it.

DAY 93, LETTER 93

Dawn M. Nothwehr

Dear President Biden, Vice President Harris, and Members of the 117th Congress,

This Earth Day, I offer you wisdom from Saint Francis of Assisi, the patron of ecology. Before writing "The Canticle of the Creatures," he announced: "I wish to compose a new hymn about the Lord's creatures, of which we make daily use, without which we cannot live, and with which the human race greatly offends its Creator." Thus, he praised God for the wonders of the natural world, from "Sir Brother Sun" to "Sister Mother Earth who sustains and governs us":

> Most High, all-powerful, good Lord,
> Yours are the *praises*, *the glory*, and *the honor*, and all *blessing*,
> To You alone, Most High, do they belong,
> and no human is worthy to mention Your name.
> *Praised be You, my Lord*, with all *Your creatures*…
> (Umbrian Italian: *Laudato Si', mi signore*)

> " *All people of goodwill are called to contemplate God's creation . . .*

Saint Francis sang his Canticle amid war, political strife, and economic upheaval—all condemned in its later verses. He confronted those threats in positive ways that honored the integral ecology and dignity of the whole creation. Thus, the Canticle is primarily a call to conversion: to eliminating the causes of war, promoting equality, and caring for God's creations—human and other kind.

In *Laudato Si'* ("on care for our common home") 139, Pope Francis echoed Saint Francis' exhortation: "When we speak of the 'environment,' what we really mean is a relationship existing between nature and the society which lives in it. …We are part of nature…We are faced…with one complex crisis which is both social and environmental." Pope Francis insists: "Strategies for a solution demand an integrated approach to combating poverty, restoring dignity to the excluded, and at the same time protecting nature."

All people of goodwill are called to contemplate God's creation, and then make personal moral, social, political, and economic changes to restore and sustain creation. I urge you to embrace today's "climate emergency" as an opportunity for overhauling our nation's infrastructure, creating jobs, and building a clean energy economy. For those intentions, let us pray with Saint Francis: "give me true faith, certain hope, and perfect charity, sense and knowledge, Lord, that I may carry out Your holy and true command. Amen."

Dear President Biden, Vice President Harris, and Members of the 117th Congress,

Thank you for undertaking major initiatives aimed at transforming our nation's socioeconomic structures and redressing centuries of injustice against marginalized communities. Amid your push for a transformative agenda, there have been numerous calls for compromise and bipartisanship so as to heed voices that offer a different vision for the nation. Bipartisanship and compromise are good models of governance in democratic nations, and they are often necessary strategies. But when bipartisanship and compromise become absolute ideals, they run the risk of empowering the very voices that seek to maintain an oppressive status quo.

Writing in the context of extreme economic inequality, the author of the Epistle of James (2:1–7) notes that God chose those who are poor in the eyes of the world and is partial to those who have been discriminated against. This text suggests that justice is about reversing existing structures and practices that favor the wealthy and ensuring that every individual and community can live with dignity and have sufficient resources to flourish.

> *... do not sacrifice a transformative agenda on the altar of bipartisanship.*

I urge you to forge ahead with your commitment to justice, with support from across the aisle, but even without it when necessary. Please be attentive to calls for bipartisanship, but do not sacrifice a transformative agenda on the altar of bipartisanship.

As you continue the work of restoring the moral fabric of our nation, please set a high bar for what qualifies as just and moral, and do not let the past four years serve as the measure of what is acceptable. I urge you not to let the morality of your policies and practices be defined by past policies, but by the values of compassion, empathy, and respect for everyone. Pursue your highest ideals, even if you fail at times. Transformative change requires that the measure of what is good is that which is ideal and envisions a different future, not just what is good enough.

Dear President Biden, Vice President Harris, and Members of the 117th Congress,

It is time to declare anti-Blackness a national emergency. The interminable lethal police attacks on Black bodies manifestly reveal the state of the emergency.

What we are witnessing across the U.S. on a seemingly daily basis is about more than white privilege. It is about more than whether or not certain persons or police are racist, or anti-racist for that matter. Rather, it is about anti-Blackness.

It is past time that the U.S. confronts the truth that American exceptionalism—the deeply rooted social construct to protect whiteness at all costs—depends on a fundamental narrative of anti-Blackness. This narrative projects the Black body as inherently threatening and violent, practically more beastly than human.

This anti-Black narrative has penetrated our collective psyche. It explains the almost instinctive tendency of some individuals—even those who otherwise consider themselves nonracist—to call police on Black people engaging in ordinary human activities. And research shows how anti-Blackness insinuates itself in the police community.

That Black people are disproportionately trapped in the violence of poverty—with its social comorbidities of inadequate health care, substandard housing, and insufficient educational and employment opportunities—is no accident.

What then are we to do—especially at a time when we are politically divided, and race-related anger and frustration stoke the cycle of anti-Black violence?

Presidents since the early nineteenth century have declared national emergencies as imperative responses to critical threats to America's security and well-being. Taking this step now could actuate:

- A national platform for historians, educators, political scientists, and thought and faith leaders to lead a reckoning with anti-Blackness and its consequences.
- An urgent plan to address and help eliminate U.S. poverty and its social comorbidities.
- A shifting of funding priorities from community police to community responders in recognition that not every emergency call requires law enforcement.

We must confront this deadly national crisis immediately, committedly, and meaningfully. A national emergency is a minimal step needed to address the scourge of anti-Blackness. Our very lives and the well-being of our communities and this nation depend on it.

Dear President Biden, Vice President Harris, and Members of the 117th Congress,

Two decades ago, like millions of people before me, I emigrated to a country that many see as a place of promises and freedoms. Yet many others experience it as a place of dispossessions and exclusions. Convinced that there is a way to rule without reproducing their suffering, today I do not want you to learn from me, but from one of your compatriots: an American who undertook a reverse migration and can help us illuminate this alternative path.

Rabbi Marshall Meyer was a native New Yorker who moved to Argentina, my homeland, and joined local struggles during the 1970s, when a genocidal dictatorship was providing a service: it was keeping the Cold War cold in the North by heating the South. Thirty thousand voices who believed in a better and just world were kidnapped, tortured, raped, and murdered because they were categorized as enemies of "Western Christian civilization." Rabbi Meyer became a member of the human rights commission that went underground to investigate the crimes against humanity.

> *…justice should be pursued by actively witnessing injustice…*

Acknowledging his privilege as an American, he was the first to leave the meetings. If he was not taken, other members were safe to return home.

Rabbi Meyer was inspired as an activist by his mentor, Rabbi Abraham Joshua Heschel, who marched with the Rev. Dr. Martin Luther King Jr. in Selma after escaping the Holocaust. Influenced by his practice of communal weekly readings of the Hebrew Bible, Rabbi Meyer persuasively and persistently encouraged his communities to interpret the commandment, "Justice, justice you shall pursue" (Deuteronomy 16:20), in conjunction with the voice of the prophet: "You are my witness" (Isaiah 44:8). He understood that justice should be pursued by actively witnessing injustice and fighting for structural changes that would dismantle those oppressions even at the risk of personal safety and comfort.

I encourage you to take inspiration from your own compatriot and rule by actively witnessing injustice. You better than anyone in the country have the chance to disarm structures of dehumanization. This is not an easy task. But as Rabbi Meyer used to quote in the name of Rabbi Tarfon: "It is not your duty to finish the work, but you are not free to neglect it" (Pirkei Avot 2:16).

Dear President Biden, Vice President Harris, and Members of the 117th Congress,

Salam, peace.

The Qur'an teaches that those who possess surplus in wealth and power must fulfill the entitlements of the impoverished and powerless. God instructs those who ask, "What are they to spend [to help others]?" that they should give away their "surplus" (2:219). They are to equitably and predictably distribute resources in excess of their needs so that such resources "do not remain in perpetual circulation among the wealthy among [them]" (59:7).

The God fearing recognize that all surplus wealth contains an "entitlement for the petitioner and the dispossessed" (51:19). It is an "obligation from God" (9:60) to mitigate the scarcity of others with one's own surplus.

> *…we are custodians of a surplus generated, mined, and cultivated over generations…*

The charitable spending or "purification" (9:11) of excess resources is a cornerstone of American Muslim religious practice. All prophets, we believe, came to instruct humanity in the "acts of welfare" (21:73) whereby inward piety could be lived out through equitable and just material relations in the community and between communities. "Goodness," the Qur'an instructs, is not "whether you turn your faces towards the east or the west [in ritual]." Rather, true righteousness and piety involve "the turning over of much-loved property to the kinspeople and to the kinless, to the deprived and the displaced, to the petitioner and the enslaved" (2:177).

America is blessed with a surplus. As a nation, we have far more than we need—be it food, microchips, or vaccines. This wealth has not come to us through our own labors alone. Rather, we are custodians of a surplus generated, mined, and cultivated over generations, through the suffering of the enslaved and through the labors, talents, and possessions of those far beyond our territorial borders. Such wealth, the Qur'an instructs, is to be "restored" to "the deprived and the displaced" (59:7). It is to be set aside for "the needy emigrants who were deprived of their homes and their properties" and those who have come to us "seeking [a share] from God's surplus" (59:8) through their own exertion.

I ask you to remember the immutable entitlements of "the petitioner and the dispossessed" (51:19). May we thrive together, *āmīn*.

Dear President Biden, Vice President Harris, and Members of the 117th Congress,

To be alive is to be acutely aware that we are mortal—yet too many of us walk the corridors of power with the arrogance of immortality. Did this virus turn the world upside down? Or do we see more clearly the lies we swallowed for decades? The sins of disaster capitalism are etched onto our bodies, a deadly game of smoke and mirrors meant to leave us fatigued, immobile, and impotent.

Mr. President, do you look around at our country—with its collapsing economic system, pharaonic hoarding of wealth, failing schools, the sham we call health care, the daily wanton murder of our Black brothers and sisters, the weapons unleashed against millions here and around the world—and ask: is this my legacy?

There is one sacred word I draw on today, and that word is the Arabic *kun*, "be." *Be* who this shattered world needs you to be, Mr. President. The divine call of creation and imagination that brought the world into being through one word, "Be" (Qur'an 2:117), is a sacred gift that lies deep within each of us. The legacy of this call is our astounding power to re-create at every moment.

> **Be *who this shattered world needs you to be ...***

Be revolutionary, Mr. President. Call into being a just world. This is not the time to reach across the aisle and shake hands with plutocrats, racists, and warmongers, to try to breathe life into our nation alongside people who know only how to deal death. What we require today are extraordinary acts of imagination and creation. Our institutions failed us because they were never built to offer every human being our God-given right to re-create ourselves. Abolitionist organizer Mariame Kaba tells us that "every vision is also a map." We must imagine our way out of punitive institutions—the neoliberal economy, policing, the criminal punishment system—that rely on the systematic oppression of many to grotesquely enrich a few. We must create our way into new collective structures that see each of us as God's beloved creation.

Listen deeply to the visionaries, Mr. President. They are young in spirit, and they are the future. Empower them, fund them, work alongside them. Let us stop dealing death and embrace the life-giving force of *Be*.

DAY 99, LETTER 99

Gay L. Byron

Dear President Biden, Vice President Harris, and Members of the 117th Congress,

In 1964, Mrs. Fannie Lou Hamer drew a line in the sand with the words: "I'm sick and tired of being sick and tired." Later in 1971, at the founding of the National Women's Political Caucus, she painted a vision for humanity and democracy: "Nobody's free till everybody's free." These words of outrage and hope inspire me to write this open letter. Ancestors like Mrs. Hamer taught me that raising my voice and taking action are the least I can do on behalf of those who are invisible, disenfranchised, and pushed to the margins.

This letter takes the form of a prayer. The prophet Jeremiah prayed in his letter to the exiles in Babylon (29:1–14). The apostle Paul prayed in his letter to the Philippians (1:3–11). The preacher Rev. Dr. Martin Luther King Jr. closed his "Letter from a Birmingham Jail" by alluding to the "long prayers" he poured out for the cause of justice. So hear now my prayer as you work together in seeking political resolve, spiritual fortitude, and uncompromising wisdom:

> **So hear now my prayer as you work together...**

Eternal Most Gracious Holy One, I pray for all elected officials of this nation. May they lead beyond political ideologies and deliver policies and opportunities that reflect the hopes and dreams of each human being of this nation. May they recognize the places in the Constitution still in need of amendment and confess the original sins of this country: violence, slavery, stolen lands and legacies, displacement, racism, sexism, classism, militarism, and more. May they repent for the roles they have played in perpetuating these sins through silence, filibusters, collusion, fear, confusion, miseducation, and more. May they surround themselves with constituents, communities of honest engagement, and spiritual guides who will hold them accountable for building equitable infrastructures, living wages, accessible health care, and safe streets. As these leaders honor their oaths of office, may they receive your forgiveness and know that they are surrounded by a great cloud of witnesses—our ancestors and all people of faith and good conscience—who expect, demand, and pray for something more over these next four years. May they be haunted and humbled by the spirit and the words of Mrs. Fannie Lou Hamer: "Nobody's free till everybody's free." Hear my prayer. Amen.

Dear President Biden, Vice President Harris, and Members of the 117th Congress,

On this, the 100th day of the Biden administration, I recall its first moments: Standing at the West Front of the U.S. Capitol on January 20, 2021, President Biden called on us to unite. In the face of a convergence of crises, the president implored: "We must meet this moment as the United States of America…let us start afresh. All of us. Let us listen to one another. Hear one another. See one another. Show respect to one another."

We, the contributors to the American Values, Religious Voices campaign, have taken up this call. On each of the last 99 days, we have written to you as scholars of religion from across the country to share values and perspectives from our diverse traditions and experiences. Each writer's vision for America is unique. Yet, united, our message is clear. We urge you to pursue justice: racial justice, environmental justice, and economic justice. We urge you to build trust, equity, and respect for all. We urge you to govern and to lead with hope, wisdom, and a commitment to truth and the democratic process.

> *This is a beginning for us, as individuals and as a nation …*

This letter marks the end of our 100-day project. Yet this is still a beginning for the Biden administration and the 117th Congress. This is a beginning for us, as individuals and as a nation, to envision what we can be and to work to bring about that vision.

At moments like this, I am reminded of the Jewish holiday of Yom Kippur. This annual fall ritual, which Jews read about in last week's Torah portion (Leviticus 16:29–34), brings us together, united as a community. We acknowledge and reflect upon our actions over the past year and resolve to do better in the coming year.

Doing so divides time in two. There is what was. There is what will be.

What will be—the future—is ours to shape. Like Yom Kippur, this requires communal ownership of the work to be done: this is the work outlined in these 100 letters. United in purpose and in our diversity, we can acknowledge the past. United, we can meet the challenges of our moment and truly start afresh.

THE
LETTERS
★ IN PRACTICE ★

Putting American Values, Religious Voices into Practice

By Lia C. Howard, PhD
Student Advising and Wellness
Director, University of Pennsylvania

The American Values, Religious Voices campaign in its 2017 and 2021 iterations provides an opportunity to examine the synergy between belief, belonging, and behavior. Now, even though the first 100 days of the Biden administration are long over, the project offers an open invitation to join in the action of speaking truth to power. The letters can continue to have impact as they are used to teach and inspire both reflection and social action.

The many individuals who wrote and read the letters do not share the same beliefs or religious traditions, yet they affirm commitments to shared values made more poignant by their differences. As people entered the project from diverse vantage points, they created community and a sense of belonging through their participation in this endeavor.

The scholars who contributed to the campaign engaged in a specific behavior, writing a letter—a practice that helped unite the group beyond differences in belief and belonging. Those who followed the project online took part in the daily practice of reading the letters and engaging with the social media posts. This practice of daily reading reinforced some existing beliefs and challenged others; it expanded people's horizons and brought about connection and discovery.

Values & Voices is implicitly and explicitly a community of practice.

The term "communities of practice" is gaining traction in higher education and beyond. The Minnesota chapter of Campus Compact uses the term to describe "a learning community, or collegial network, defined as 'a group of people who share interest in an area of inquiry and engage in collective learning about that issue as it relates to their work or practice. Through discussions, joint activities, and relationship building, the community of practice develops a shared and individual repertoire of resources, skills, and knowledge to use in their practice.'"

Viewing Values & Voices as a community of practice, we asked a variety of individuals—artists, educators, clergy, and political activists—to write about how the letters could be used to further their practice in their respective fields. We invite you to read their ideas, engage actively with the letters, and imagine new ways to bring the letters to life in your own areas of expertise and practice. Join our community of practice so that we can continue to exercise our shared values, together.

Using the Letters for Adult Learning

By Lesley Litman, EdD, RJE
Director, Executive MA n Jewish
Education and Instructional Support
Coordinator, Hebrew Union College–
Jewish Institute of Religion

In today's hyperconnected, eminently searchable cyber universe, where information is abundant and at our fingertips, the goal of teaching is to help learners find the significance of that information and to make meaning for how they live their lives and walk in their worlds.

This essay focuses on adult children of aging parents who inhabit multiple roles in their lives and in our connection with them. Perhaps they are learners for learning's sake, teachers seeking to grow in their understanding and practice, parents, friends, or adult children of parents. Meaning-making crosses all of the identities we inhabit, particularly when it involves deepening our understanding of and wrestling with the values we hold dear. The following are some key guidelines for enabling adult learners to dive into the American Values, Religious Voices letters:

Key Guidelines

❶ All learning is relational

Learners learn best when they feel connected to their teachers and to each other. This is true across the life span. ***Provide*** multiple opportunities for interaction and relationship building as a way to create a safe environment for risk taking in learning.

❷ Learn through inquiry

Open-ended, sophisticated questions lead to profound insights. ***Help*** your learners cultivate questions that lead to multiple possible answers and open up more questions that in turn invite learners to dig even deeper into the materials and into themselves.

❸ Make teaching learner-centered

What is on the mind of your learners? What's intriguing them or bothering them? Effective adult learning experiences begin with the concerns and life tasks of the learner. ***Choose*** the letters and teaching methodology that respond to your learners' interests.

Using the Letters for Adult Learning

④ Close reading and careful listening are based on dialogue

Dialogue happens between learners. The letters are also in dialogue with each other through both values and themes represented.

⑤ Learn through reflection

All learners benefit from the opportunity to step back at the end of the learning session and consider what new insights, questions, and life-significance they have gained from the learning.

The Values & Voices letters provide myriad opportunities to bring these guidelines to life in these times in which dialogue, listening, and reflection are so significant in healing a polarized world.

USING THE FRAMEWORK OF VALUES IN TENSION

EXAMPLE 1

The Role of Government

Yehuda Kurtzer (Letter 37) and **Joshua D. Garroway** (Letter 38) raise questions about the degree and purpose of the government's involvement in the life of citizens from a Jewish perspective, drawing on two commonly held Jewish values: responsibility for the greater good and our inalienable right to be free, respectively.

EXAMPLE 2

Reproductive Justice

Jennifer L. Koosed (Letter 43) and **Shawnee M. Daniels-Syke**s (Letter 44) draw on different yet closely connected values that cross their faith traditions (Jewish and Catholic, respectively) to reach different value-based conclusions.

In each of these examples, the following questions enable learners to enact the guidelines listed on pages 147 and 148.

- Even if you do not agree with the conclusion the author draws, what rings true for you in the letter?

- What do you question in the letter that most resonates for you?

- How is it possible for two scholars from the same religious faith or two closely connected values to reach such different conclusions?

- How does the letter that least resonates enrich or inform your understanding of your own perspective?

- In what part of your life does this conversation most matter? Why and how?

One might also choose a particular theme in which values may not be in tension but, rather, enrich and deepen the learner's understanding of the theme. Themes can be framed by issue (such as the environment or dealing with pain and grief) or by value (such as hope, truth, justice, or love). To help you create connections between themes and values in the letters, use the Thematic Values Tally (pages 8–11), the Values pages (pages 37, 49, 61, 73, 85, 97, 109, 121, 133), and the Subject Index (pages 168–75).

Ultimately, as the organizers of the American Values, Religious Voices campaign point out, studying these letters together unleashes the potential to help learners create dialogue and healing, celebrate our glorious diversity, and make sense of the world we live in today, while shining a light on the world we want to create for tomorrow.

Notes

★

Spiritual Reading

By Rabbi Debra J. Robbins
Temple Emanu-El, Dallas, TX

Reading a Values & Voices letter feels like reading a passage of sacred scripture. Each word is carefully chosen (some perhaps even divinely inspired). Each phrase invites the reader to reflect, interpret, and then engage with the text and the world. This kind of reading is countercultural. It is not about racing through a post or scanning for a speaker's sound bite. It is about being still long enough to allow words to saturate the soul. It is about feeling the words: with our hands as we write, with our hearts as we sit with them, and with our bodies as we strive to make their challenges our own. Ritual can transform ordinary time into a holy moment, just as reading a letter can become a sacred encounter. Becoming a spiritual reader takes patience and practice, and structure can help make it a holy habit.

Prepare

A place. Make the space tidy. As the poet Billy Collins says in his "Advice to Writers" (in *Sailing Alone Around the Room*): "Clean the place as if the Pope were on his way. Spotlessness is the niece of inspiration."

A pencil and notebook. I recommend this over the computer, to allow the words to flow in a way that is different from how we type on a keyboard or text with our thumbs.

A timer. An alarm or meditation app on your phone works well. Make sure everything else is turned off.

Engage

Read. First, read the letter aloud, slowly. Giving voice to the diversity of voices in the book allows the reader to encounter them differently, manifesting the project's goals. If you prefer, listen to the audio or watch the video.

Second, select a phrase, three to five words, a snippet of scripture, a piece of a quote, a question posed in the letter.

Write. Date the page. Copy the phrase onto the paper. Select a prompt from below, and don't waste time trying to decide which one. Set the timer for five minutes. Write. Don't edit, don't erase, don't criticize your words or judge yourself, just keep writing.

- **What images, experiences, emotions does this phrase evoke?**
- **How do these words speak to your moral imagination?**
- **What sparkles and why?**

Sit. You may be inclined to reverse the order—but please don't. Writing and *then* sitting can lead to deeper reflection and ownership of the phrase. Set the timer for five minutes. Settle into a dignified seated position. Take a few deep breaths. Try not to think about "meditation" or how to "use" the letter or your written words. Maybe close your eyes. Repeat the phrase, over and over again. See the words in your mind. When you get distracted, take another deep breath and come back to the phrase. Allow the letter, the phrase, your own written reflection this time to percolate, germinate, integrate

Give thanks. Take a moment to offer gratitude: to the author of the letter, to yourself for doing this work, and if appropriate, to The One We Call By Many Names and Know in Infinite Ways, for wisdom and insight, courage and compassion, faith and hope and healing.

★

Embodying Religious Wisdom

By Nirinjan Kaur Khalsa-Baker, PhD

Senior Instructor, Loyola Marymount University

The trauma of the past few years has been exhausting—waking up in isolation, separated from family and friends as a result of a global pandemic; escalating political polarization, environmental devastation, abuses of power, and acts of violence rooted in racism, sexism, and xenophobia. The American Values, Religious Voices campaign serves as a reminder that we are not alone or separate, that our diverse religious traditions pull from the deep wellspring of wisdom, nurtured by shared values of love, service, compassion, and care. The letters offer a balm for the soul, a return to the heart, a call to accountability and integrity during these troubled times.

In the first 100 days after the presidential inauguration in 2017 and again in 2021, each letter came into my inbox in the early morning and was the first thing I read before beginning my workday. These letters served as daily reminders to pause, breathe, and reflect upon the state of our world, contemplate our vision for humanity, and discern our role in fighting for a better tomorrow. Reading and reflecting upon the religious wisdom shared in these letters became a daily practice.

The Sikh, Yoga, and Indian traditions teach the importance of embodying wisdom as a daily practice to transform how we think, see, and act in the world. Daily embodied practices, or **sadhana**, such as meditation (**simran**), repetition (**japa**), and contemplative readings (**vichar**), allow wisdom to become enshrined in the heart, mind, and soul, guiding our actions in daily life.

Take a minute and try this practice by first grounding in your body.

1 **Inhale** deeply and exhale completely.

2 Continue to **breathe** long and deep.

3 **Relax** your eyes and soften your gaze.

4 As you breathe, **connect** with your senses and the sensations in your body.

5 **Feel** the earth below your feet.

6 **Listen** to the sounds around you, take in the smells, and allow these sensations without judgment.

7 **Notice** the feeling of the air coming in and out of your nose.

8 **Feel** your chest and belly rising and falling.

9 Begin to **scan** your body, bringing your breath to dissolve any place that may hold tension.

From this embodied state of present awareness, open this book to any passage and take in the words on the page. Allow yourself to read and listen with love in your heart, pausing to contemplate or meditate on the words or lines that speak to you. Hold these words with you as you go about your day, allowing the words of wisdom to become a living meditation.

Breathing-in-wisdom

Through the practices of breathing-in wisdom on a daily basis, we are reminded to hold ourselves and our leaders accountable. The chorus of diverse wisdom traditions sung through these letters allows us to see the world through multiple perspectives, described by the Jains as **anekantavada**. As a psychological practice, it allows us to see the multifaceted nature of reality and have compassion for different ways of knowing and being.

When we stay connected to the wisdom of our traditions through compassion and present-moment awareness, we broaden how we see the world and how we embrace each other. Together, we expand our horizon of what is possible by calling out injustices and calling in our commitment to serve one another as a global **sangha** or **sangat,** a beloved community.

★

Collective Action & Political Activism

By Reverend Dr. Liz Theoharis
Co-Chair, Poor People's Campaign;
Director, Kairos Center for Religions,
Rights, and Social Justice at Union
Theological Seminary

For too long, our society has looked to the rich and powerful for answers to the problems the nation faces.

But rather, it is the collective action of those most impacted by injustice—together in a broad fusion movement with people of all walks of life—that can bring about a moral revolution of values and improve life for the poor and for everyone.

From abolition to the industrial union movement of the 1930s to the Civil Rights Movement, from the Underground Railroad to unemployment councils and freedom rides, people on the receiving end of injustice did not wait to be saved, but took heroic action born out of necessity.

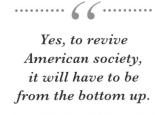

Yes, to revive American society, it will have to be from the bottom up.

Today, there is a freedom railroad rumbling underground, all around us. Look for evidence of such rumblings as you read the American Values, Religious Voices letters. This railroad has stops in the towns and cities winning policy victories as people proclaim "We can't breathe" and "We won't be silent until Black lives matter." Look for evidence in the Amazon warehouses, Starbucks stores, and fast-food restaurants where low-wage workers are organizing for better wages and conditions. Look for evidence in the immigrant communities that are protecting themselves against ICE raids and crying out for papers, not crumbs; in the places where people are winning moratoriums on water and utility shutoffs; in the housing developments and hospitals where thousands are demanding that housing and health care are human rights.

Yes, to revive American society, it will have to be from the bottom up. This is true from history, as we read in these letters from a diverse group of leaders from across the nation. But as these letters also make clear: our sacred texts declare that policies that do not protect the rights of the poor and put the cause of the wealthy first are evil. Change must come from the bottom up.

As you read these letters, I encourage you to:

 Explore the biblical and theological foundations from your faith tradition and from others included in these letters for building a social justice movement from the bottom up.

 Identify the systemic injustices and moral issues impacting your community and listen to what these letters are saying must be done to confront inequality and injustice.

 Get involved in organizations, congregations, and campaigns working to address the issues that are raised in the letters and that you are concerned about in your own life and community.

 Partner with those most impacted by social, racial, economic, gender, and environmental injustice as you deepen your involvement in the work of social transformation.

There is much work to do.

We have been given our marching orders by the authors of these 100 letters, written to the thousands who are taking action together from the communities they represent. As Ella Josephine Baker challenges us:

"WE WHO BELIEVE IN FREEDOM CANNOT REST UNTIL IT COMES."

★

Civic Organizing & Political Activism for Gen Z

By Charissa (Rissa) Howard
First-year student, University of Pennsylvania

For decades to come, my generation will be known as the one that took action. In the midst of some of the largest threats the world has known, from climate change to a global pandemic, we are fighting back. We volunteer on political campaigns, phone-banking and text-banking for candidates that matter to us. We use social media to spread awareness and organize movements. We take to the streets, assembling school walkouts and protests, for organizations such as the March for Our Lives movement and the Black Lives Matter movement, some of the largest in history.

We also write letters, just like the ones in this collection. Letters have become one of the most effective ways to reach those

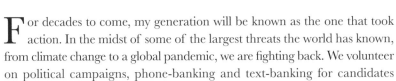

> *Letters have become one of the most effective ways to reach those across the political aisle…*

across the political aisle, as well as elected officials who often skim past the flood of emails that they receive. They remain a wonderfully effective way to convey emotion and to inspire their readers. The letters in American Values, Religious Voices did just that for me. Here are a few action items that I hope other young people take away from these letters:

Action Items

❶ Learn from those who came before us.

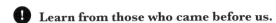

Most of these letters include quotes that shine as beacons of hope, whether from religious texts or from leaders such as Dr. Martin Luther King Jr., Gloria Anzaldúa, Howard Thurman, and Fannie Lou Hamer. The words can serve as reminders that others who came before suffered trials but had the audacity to fight and write their way toward a better future.

❗ Cultivate dialogue across difference. This is the most vital way that we can combat the intense division that is plaguing our country right now. The collection serves as a model for what such dialogue can look like. Each letter—whose authors represent a variety of different perspectives—is filled with a spirit of resilience. By reading and interacting with opinions and outlooks different from our own, we can continue to cultivate and tend to American democracy.

❗ Speak your truth. Just like all of these letter writers, find what you are passionate about and speak out about it. Weave in your personal experiences and take action against that which is unfair. Transform your despair into determination.

Transform your despair into determination!

One of my lifelong favorite quotes comes from the poet Maya Angelou: "Hope and fear cannot occupy the same space," she wrote. "Invite one to stay." My prayer for my generation is that we open our hearts to hope and close the door to fear. Take these letters, the words of those who came before, and your dreams for America to keep fighting for a better tomorrow.

★

Learning from the Letters about Interfaith Discourse

By Murali Balaji, PhD
Maruthi Education Consulting and
Lecturer, University of Pennsylvania

One of the core tenets of Hinduism is that the ability to learn and strive to better practice *dharma* (righteous action for the greater good) is universal, no matter one's class, education, vocation, or age.

That tenet is especially resonant today given how many people have refused to open themselves to learning, choosing instead to stay hunkered down in ideological or affinity spaces, and refusing to see the divinity in all. For many young and older Hindus alike, there is a palpable sense of frustration that Hinduism is not always welcome in interfaith discourses and coalitions to make the country a better place.

But the letters in this volume can offer a way forward. The Dharmic, Abrahamic, humanist, and Indigenous traditions to which the letter writers belong are replete with stories of resilience, restoring light, and encouraging humankind to grow. We see the resonance of our own stories in the stories of others, which makes this country stronger to fight existential threats—climate change, a global pandemic, poverty, xenophobia, and economic inequality, among others—and paves a path forward for all of us.

> " *This volume offers a way to use our scriptures as a means of civic engagement and to cast a vision for the future…*

This volume offers a way to use our scriptures as a means of civic engagement and to cast a vision for the future that is both pluralistic and equal. For years, interfaith engagement on civic issues has shut out non-Abrahamic voices. As Hindu, Buddhist, Jain, and Sikh populations and revived First Nations traditions grow in this country, such exclusion harms our efforts to become a more perfect union.

The lessons that the letter writers—academics, activists, faith leaders—teach us are relatable at every level, and the letters provide us a way to put our scriptures into action. Imagine being the child of Hindus who immigrated to this country five decades ago and who was unable to find tangible lessons on how to be a Hindu within an American context. I know that experience well, which is why I am heartened to see more Hindu organizations providing practical guidance to Hindu Americans while extending their hands in fellowship to other faith communities. I see Muslim, Sikh, Christian, humanist, and other groups doing the same. So even if the progress is measured in inches rather than in giant leaps, we are getting there.

Use these letters to spur dialogue

1 **Invite friends of diverse beliefs to read letters** from traditions that are different from their own.

2 **Ask your friends if there are any nuggets in the letters** that resonate with them or points they may want to challenge or critique. After all, interfaith engagement is not about interfaith agreement; it is about engaging as equals, even if we respectfully agree to disagree.

American Values, Religious Voices offers an example of what happens when we bring together the best of our traditions to improve our democracy. The next challenge that we all must embrace is taking these lessons to our communities in an empathetic and loving manner, without judgment, and with the greatest hope that we all share in the desire to learn and evolve.

Om Shanti, Shanti, Shanti

PRACTICE 7

Our Own Sacred, Civic Texts

By David Bradley

Philadelphia-based chaplain, arts leader, educator; Director, "Dear President Biden"

★ *Take to heart these instructions with which I charge you this day . . . Bind them as a sign on your hand and let them serve as a symbol on your forehead; Inscribe them on the doorposts of your house and on your gates.*

Excerpt from the Hebrew prayer *V'ahavta* (Deuteronomy 6:6–9)

★ *How can we encourage a politics of empathy and fairness? One just, kind, compassionate, equitable word at a time.*

Actor David Strathairn, speaking about American Values, Religious Voices

On Presidents' Day 2021, more than 300 people across three countries gathered on Zoom for "Dear President Biden," a live event featuring professional actors reading Values & Voices letters, singer-songwriters performing original songs inspired by the letters, and a town hall conversation where those gathered offered their responses. The event provided performance, ritual, testimony. It offered words in action and action sparked by words.

I've worked in theater and music for over 30 years. I've relished delving into great texts from Shakespeare and Arthur Miller. I've also been lucky to hear intimate texts from "ordinary" people, such as a 90-year-old confiding: "I don't know why you wanna talk to me, I haven't done anything," and then unfurling extraordinary experiences mapping the national forest system in the 1930s. I've witnessed new parents creating heartfelt lullabies in workshops with professional songwriters. I've learned that we each make our own great texts—the stories that shape us, the values passed on to a next generation—that mark how we live. These point to deep truths of who we are; they take on the power of the sacred. They also underscore our identities as citizens.

Our "Dear President Biden" event collaged sacred and civic texts—from ancient religious traditions, as well as from a composer for whom the letters unlocked a long-incubating song and from audience members seeking to bridge divides with their neighbors. The letters became a transformative fulcrum in a civic "whisper down the lane," where the wisdom of prophets was catalyzed by the aspirations of contemporary scholars, fueling the energies of artists, and

160

finally encouraging, as one of the participants, Oscar nominee David Strathairn said, the "compassionate, equitable" words of citizens.

Could these letters "serve as symbols," as the prayer on page 160 says, lifting our own texts and pointing to how we can speak?

What if you . . .

 Quote the letters to your elected representatives in emails and town halls—adding the letters' power to your own formidable civic engagement?

 Excerpt the letters in missives to your children or grandchildren (your own future president?), joining your lived experience of democracy with the vigor of passionate teachers and ancient activists?

 Combine the concept of the Little Library (those homemade boxes where neighbors donate books) with the Jewish tradition of the *mezuzah* (the beautifully rendered signposts housing the commandments to love God and neighbor) and design neighborhood signs, sculptures, rock gardens emblazoned with quotes from the letters?

 Make this your next book club selection, so the vibrancy of your own circle of empathy and vision can sing these ideas forward into new worlds?

 Compose a song, poem, or other piece of art inspired by one or more of the letters? (see pages 162–63)

"Rituals are important because they make explicit our implicit values," Katherine Ozment observed in her book *Grace Without God: The Search for Meaning, Purpose, and Belonging in a Secular World*. These letters offer a new civic ritual. Their very impulse—taking long-ago words to inspire new action—keeps the ritual going. That ritual continues with us. To add our own "what if." To imagine the next equitable word. To speak our own sacred, civic texts with creativity into an oh-so-ready world.

★

ORIGINAL SONG

We Are Bound

Inspired by:
Letter 1: Andrea L. Weiss
Letter 4: Marc Z. Brettler
Letter 77 (2017):
Karma Lekshe Tsomo

By Keisha Hutchins

Philadelphia-based singer-
songwriter and educator who
uses these platform to bring
attention to social justice issues

Photo: Spencer Skelly

Scan to listen.

Verse 1

I woke up breathless, in my dream
we were runnin'
Chasing something that can't be
denied
And I thought in that moment
I was glad you were with me
Cause I knew this chase could
change the tide

You said,
Be courageous, Be strong
But most of all be kind
You stood beside me
And that moment
Your freedom was bound
up in mine

Chorus

We are bound
Bound up in you
Bound up in me

We are bound
Born of one truth
That sets us free

We are bound
Bound up in me
Bound up in you

We are bound
Born of one truth
That sets us free

We are bound

Verse 2

After justice, after justice we
must chase
If we are to ever survive this place
By cherishing you I am cherishing me
And all of your love has helped me
to see

I must break open my heart
You break open yours, too
What once started with me
Now ends with you
Now ends with you

[Chorus]

Verse 3

So let's make this promise
Get down on our knees
Keep runnin' towards justice
Til we can barely breathe

And when you get tired
I'll run for you
And I know that you will run
for me, too

I'll break open my heart
You break open yours, too
What once started with me
Now ends with you
Now ends with you

[Chorus]

ORIGINAL SONG

Can't Keep Truth Locked Away

Inspired by:
Letter 3: Lisa Bowens
Letter 5: Anantanand Rambachan
Letter 17: Kimberly D. Russaw

By Ami Yares

Philadelphia-based singer-songwriter and executive director of BuildaBridge International who catalyzes music and the arts to help realize hope-infused futures

Scan to listen.

Verse 1
Unfurl the past
Like an old map
Look from we came
Look at where we're at

A path dependent
We seem to be
Our sins repeat
At the risk of losing everything

But chains can break
And bonds unbound

Chorus
We'll shake the shackles
Rattle the cage
Cause you can't keep truth
locked away
We'll shake the shackles
Rattle the cage
Cause you can't keep truth
locked away
No you can't keep truth
locked away

Verse 2
Untruth to truth
Darkness to light
Unveil the beauty
That sits between the eyes

Don't let their lies
Burden your load
Truth moves in you
And will keep you strong

Words have weight
And chains can break

[Chorus]

Bridge
You see, the people here
Got the mind to the work
Kick the dirt from the hurt
And let your love show
for the world

Words have weight
And chains can break

[Chorus]

A PRAYER
FOR OUR COUNTRY

We turn to the light of religious wisdoms to guide us through the darkness.

May we move forward with compassion and embodied wisdom.

May we build a bridge to a future that reckons with the past but refuses to resemble it.

Bring healing and reconciliation while leading the nation forward using your own moral compass.

Lead us as a country to live into new dreams with and for each other.

Keep your eye out for people who have been quietly doing the work of faith and justice.

Empower those who build community across difference.

Be encouraged, knowing the people have a mind to work.

Be strong and resolute. Act boldly and decisively.

Create the conditions for wholeness, justice, and peace for all in our midst.

This prayer was adapted from letters written by **Nirinjan Kaur Khalsa-Baker** (Letter 53), **Grace Song** (Letter 65), **Jacqueline M. Hidalgo** (Letter 45), **Corrine Carvalho** (Letter 19), **Neomi De Anda** (Letter 30), **Margaret Aymer** (Letter 23), **Katherine A. Shaner** (Letter 39), **Kimberly D. Russaw** (Letter 17), **Judith Plaskow** (Letter 10), and **Elsie R. Stern** (Letter 50)

★ ACKNOWLEDGMENTS ★

In a February 9, 2017, *Philadelphia Inquirer* article on American Values, Religious Voices campaign, Dr. Elsie R. Stern (author of 2017 Letter 100) stated: "I would love to see this project with every presidential election…I think the idea that these incredibly wise religious traditions have a lot to say to folks who have just ascended to positions of enormous power isn't specific to this moment." After the 2020 election, we decided that Elsie was right—but it would take many individuals to bring that idea to fruition.

The second Values & Voices campaign got off the ground when Rebecca Tauber agreed to become our editorial assistant and recruited two Williams College classmates: Kayla Gillman as creative assistant and Sophia Sonnenfeldt as communications assistant.

Hebrew Union College–Jewish Institute of Religion President Andrew Rehfeld encouraged the launch of the 2021 campaign, and many HUC–JIR faculty, staff, students, Board members, and alumni enthusiastically supported the project in 2017 and 2021. A devoted subscriber, Lisa Messinger, provided valuable advice and financial assistance as the campaign got started.

We received a generous grant from the Lippman Kanfer Foundation for Living Torah that enabled us to hire Gary Blatt to update our website. The grant also supported "Dear President Biden: A Presidents' Day Performance and Community Conversation." We thank moderator David Bradley; Congressman Dwight Evans; actors Taysha Canales, Angel Desai, Nilaja Sun, David Strathairn, and Michele Tauber; songwriters and performers Keisha Hutchins, Ami Yares, and Bethlehem Roberson; ASL interpreters Brandice Mazick and Donna Ellis; students Salawat Adam and Zachary Nosanchuk; producers Galea McGregor and Kate Fossner; and publicist Bryan Buttler.

Values & Voice 2021 only happened because fifty-nine 2017 authors and forty-two new scholars wrote wise and inspirational letters to our leaders in Washington. We thank them and our dedicated subscribers who read the letters day in and day out.

We are grateful to Elizabeth Scarpelli, Director of University of Cincinnati Press and Library Publisher Services, for giving us the opportunity to publish the 2021 letters. We thank all those at the University of Cincinnati Press who worked on this book: Sophie Ballah, Alex Nash, and Sarah Muncy.

To produce this book, we partnered with Dr. Lia Howard and Rebecca Tauber. Lia had the vision for the practice essays and enlisted the contributors: Murali Balaji, David Bradley, Charissa Howard, Nirinjan Kaur Khalsa-Baker, Lesley Litman, Deborah Robbins, and Reverend Dr. Liz Theoharis. Dr. Casey Bohlen's essay and the song lyrics by Keisha Hutchins and Ami Yares enhance the book and the letters' impact.

The creative team at Masters Group Design, including Claire Zellin, Benjamin Brown, and Vicki Gray-Wolfe, contributed to the design of the book. We are grateful to them and MGD's long-time collaborator, Janice Fisher, who lent her editing expertise to these pages.

We extend our heartfelt thanks and love to our families: Eric, Avi, and Jakob Cantor; Alan, Rebecca, and Ilan Tauber; and our parents Susan and Norman Weinberger and Ruth and Marty Weiss.

In his 2017 letter, Murali Balaji asked, "What can we do to create light together?" We thank everyone who joined with us to create more light through the American Values, Religions Voices campaign.

Andrea L. Weiss & Lisa M. Weinberger

Scriptural Index

Subject Index

Names highlighted in red indicate the 2021 American Values, Religious Voices letter writers.

K

Kaba, Mariame: 142

Kassam, Tazim: 122, 125

Kassam, Zayn: 110, 109, 111

Kemp, Joel: 97–98, 100

Khalsa-Baker, Nirinjan Kaur: 16, 86, 89, 121, 152, 164

kindness: 8, 27, 40, 46, 92, 94, 153, 160, 162

King, Martin Luther Jr: 27, 55, 58, 66–67, 132, 140, 143, 156

kinship: 21, 66, 89

Kizenko, Nadia: 26, 34

Koller, Aaron: 86, 88

Koltun-Fromm, Naomi: 98–99

Koosed, Jennifer: 74, 77, 133, 148

Korean War: 72

Kraus, Matthew: 74, 83

Kurtzer, Yehuda: 62, 69, 148

L

Lady Gaga: 117

Latin: 55, 57

Latina/o/x: 60, 63, 113

Laudato Si': 44, 57, 93, 137

leadership: 21, 28, 33, 36, 42, 47, 52, 54, 59, 60, 65, 69, 72, 76, 99, 101, 104, 112, 126, 131, 136

"least of these": 41, 53, 64

Lent: 115–16; Lenten: 17; Orthodox Lent: 116

Lewis, John: 131–32

Lewis, Karoline: 16, 74, 76, 97

LGBTQ: 72, 93, 130

liberty: 12, 52, 70–72, 87, 89, 111, 131; Liberty Bell: 52

Liew, Tat-siong Benny: 50, 57

light: 18, 31, 35, 43, 63, 72, 87–89, 131, 149, 158, 163–64

Lincoln, Abraham: 20, 40, 46, 54

Lopez, Jennifer: 117

love: 11–12, 21–22, 28–30, 40, 48, 51–52, 56, 58, 63, 69, 76, 79–80, 94, 97, 100, 103, 111, 113, 115–16, 119–20, 129, 131, 141, 149, 152–53, 161–62

M

MacGregor, Neil: 115

Marbury, Herbert Robinson: 13, 86, 91

marginalized: 47–48, 78, 107, 116, 118, 130, 138

Mary: 42, 63, 115, 124

Massingale, Bryan: 37, 122, 129

Meir, Rabbi: 70

mercy: 11, 29, 33, 39, 53–54, 56, 58, 61, 94, 111

Merton, Thomas: 119

Meyer, Eric Daryl: 21, 86, 93

Meyer, Rabbi Marshall: 140

migrant: 32, 60, 111

Mikva, Rachel: 38, 44, 61

Miller, Anna: 122, 130, 133

Miller, Arthur: 160

Miriam: 63, 75

Mormons: 22

Morrison, Toni: 114

Moses: 27, 36, 47, 63, 84, 90, 104, 107, 120

Mott, Lucretia: 119

Muhammad: 33, 39, 95

Muslim: 19, 22, 33, 39, 54, 111, 127, 141, 158

N

Nadella, Raj: 37, 134, 138

Nanko-Fernández, Carmen: 26, 32

Native American: 40

neighbor: 13, 21, 48, 65, 69, 78, 93, 112, 123, 129, 160; neighborhood: 12, 66; love for the neighbor: 12, 21, 48, 51–52

New Testament: 67, 108, 113, 123

Ngwa, Kenneth: 21, 98, 107, 109

nonviolence: 67, 119, 127, 136

Nothwehr, Dawn: 61, 134, 137

★ ★ ★

The American Values, Religious Voices campaign, with its website and social media outlets (@ValuesandVoices), is the result of a unique partnership between a biblical scholar and a graphic designer who joined forces after the 2016 presidential election to start a public dialogue about American values.

Rabbi Andrea L. Weiss, PhD, is Jack, Joseph and Morton Mandel Provost and associate professor of Bible at the Hebrew Union College – Jewish Institute of Religion.

Lisa M. Weinberger is founder and creative director of Masters Group Design, a design and branding studio in Philadelphia, Pennsylvania, and Tulsa, Oklahoma.

Lia C. Howard is a political scientist who serves as the Student Advising and Wellness Director at the University of Pennsylvania's Stavros Niarchos Foundation Paideia Program.

Rebecca Tauber is a journalist covering local politics for Colorado Public Radio and Denverite, and editorial assistant on the 2021 Values & Voices campaign and book.

Scan to visit the campaign website:
valuesandvoices.com